Alabama Crimson Tide

1967 and the Undercurrents of Integration

The First Five—Before the Season Changed

BY ANDREW PERNELL

DORRANCE
PUBLISHING C(
EST. 1920
PITTSBURGH, PENNSYLVANIA

The contents of this work, including, but not limited to, the accuracy of events, people, and places depicted; opinions expressed; permission to use previously published materials included; and any advice given or actions advocated are solely the responsibility of the author, who assumes all liability for said work and indemnifies the publisher against any claims stemming from publication of the work.

Dorrance Publishing Co
585 Alpha Drive
Suite 103
Pittsburgh, PA 15238

Visit our website at *www.dorrancebookstore.com*

ISBN: 978-1-6495-7270-7
eISBN: 978-1-6495-7774-0

FOREWORD

By Brian Andre Pernell

I am, in part, what I am today because of an existential and kindred belonging to a virtuous spirit. I am able to stand or kneel, with a measure of virtue, only because of a foundational reassurance that the just will prevail. A foundation that is possible because of one's life course and all the sundry hurdles along the path. I am of the belief that there are few things comparable to a great example.

A child longs for the reflection in the mirror to bear some familiarity, to present itself some semblance of meaning, a connection, albeit greatness or merely belonging, the desire is all the same. When a child finds that, he finds himself. To have found and to be proud of a lineage that has risen and overcome the enormity of circumstance is to hold one's head high, shoulders back, chest out, innately equipped, too, with the apparatuses to overcome. To know the antiquity, yet, to witness such grit and elevation despite it, is magical to a son. When a father's example begets hope, that hope then becomes a beacon not only for his seed, but for all those within the sphere of influence of that seed. I'd surmise that a father's example is a gift that keeps on giving. Sometimes, if we're lucky, we're gifted a collection of truths to enjoy at our fingertips for eternity.

The eloquent writing that you will soon read in this book reveals the nature of the man that I know as Pops—my dad. This proud son impresses upon you that this book affords a most poignant insight, a snapshot into his character, a revelation into the essence of a man, during a most tumultuous time in his young life, his truth. Though I have heard accounts of the events revealed in the book on occasion through the years, I am beyond delighted at the untethered style and grace and composition presented in this work.

The writing takes you on a journey throughout the emotional roller coaster that history has recorded as an austere time in America's history; specifically, it affords the curious eye a snapshot behind the scenes of a blueblood football program that is the Alabama Crimson Tide in the early 1960's. Many of us may have pondered what it would be like to be a black athlete during this era, an era laden with troubled times for people of color, well—my Dad lived it, and through a series of cathartic revelations and an iron clad memory, Pops takes us on a journey through his young life, the injustices, heartache, trials, tribulation, sacrifices, and ultimately—triumphs.

Ponder these words as you begin your journey through this captivating memoir:

> Life is funny this way. There is a time to be born and a time to die. All that lies between is a reflection and the impression of you and its impact and those things that shaped it, life that is. Perhaps the journey bears greater weight than the destination. Interesting are the scales of justice this way. To be born in a time of vitriol that should have merely borne innocence and peace and sanctuary, but instead, it bore hardships, travesty, and missed opportunities, is indeed unjust.
>
> The cumulative weight of life's unfortunate experiences, likened unto the notches on the proverbial belt and feelings on the proverbial sleeve, the tattered clothes oftentimes tell the story of the man. Some argue that the true measure of a man is how he responds in times of adversity. Others may argue that the measure of a man is how he might treat those that can do nothing for him. Both arguments are not only equally valid, but true. My Pops has been measured on both accounts and the measurements have proven to be exact and true.
>
> The image of the man in the mirror not only reflects the man, but a deeper look at the image *reveals* the man. Does the deeper look into the mirror reveal one of strength,

courage, perseverance, and hope or does it reveal one of weakness, cowardice, inconstancy, and hopelessness? History has judged and revealed, with certainty, that my Pops is a man of strength, courage, perseverance, and hope.

Who is the judge and what would the mirror say to the reflection in it? What is the weight of strength and courage and hope, and perseverance? For what is the cost and weight of hate and fear and deterrence? What do the scales of justice say? As the man in the mirror ponders, right has one side—history will reflect the one-sidedness of right.

Let the scales of justice reflect that my dad, a proud black man, now a father, still a son of custodial excellence, husband and man of God, living in the consciousness of today's America—an unfortunate replica of her old self, and a seed of the deep South—has risen above and overcome a unique set of circumstances in a unique place, during a most tumultuous time in American history. Let the scales of justice reflect that this writing is a representation of the absolute truth, which captures an amazing journey of trials, tribulations, triumphs, strength, perseverance, and redemption. I ask God that you will allow the man in the mirror to experience your abundant grace for taking and overcoming the road less traveled, staying faithful, and being impactful along the way.

This book is an easy read; however, it causes the reader to be reflective and considerate in regards to *the* truth of the presentation. You may even find it controversial, because the truth oftentimes leads to controversy when it is unadulterated. Those who value the truth will find this book a must read.

This book is dedicated to my parents, Leslie and Mary Pernell, who sacrificed and allowed me to take risks; to my wife, Chelsea, who encouraged me to get on with it; and to my three sons, Brian Andre Pernell, Leland Christopher Wilson, and Brian Christopher Pernell, who have made me proud to be their dad.

CONTENTS

THE PREFACE

"Forasmuch as many have taken in hand to set forth in order a declaration of those things which are most surely believed among us, even as they delivered them unto us...it seemed to me also, having had perfect understanding of all things from the very first to write unto thee in order...that thou mightiest know the certainty of those things, wherein thou hast been instructed."

(Luke 1:1-4, KJV).

Over the years, quite a few people have written about the story of The First Five. There are several versions of the integration story and there are many commentaries on those University of Alabama Crimson Tide days. To my knowledge, none of us First Five who *was* actually there as participants have recorded the events of the times as *we experienced* them. I was the only one of the first five who *survived* and returned after the spring A-Day game of 1967; therefore, my account of events may be more comprehensive and enriching than others' accounts. This book, I would wager, presents the historicity of those things of which I write, more accurately than any other written account.

The title of this book is a bit of a spin-off of Prof. John David Briley's book, *Career in Crisis, Paul Bear Bryant and the 1971 Season of Change.* Prof. Briley's book shed some light on the season *before* the change, but with an emphasis on the changing season itself and its aftermath; however, the focus of this book highlights significant and relevant events *before* the season changed, interspersed with *my commentary on race*—which lies at the heart of this memorialization.

It is almost impossible to write a book such as this, on the integration of sports at the University of Alabama in 1967, without discussing the multi-faceted construct of race, and I will not attempt such a feat in this book. If we were five white walk-ons in 1967, I am quite sure that there would have been no notice taken. There *were* white walk-ons in the fall of 1967, but there is no notoriety regarding their efforts; that's the way it should have been with The First Five in 1967, but *segregation* created The First Five.

I am writing neither from an "all was well" position nor an "it wasn't that bad" minimization. I am not writing from a standpoint of placation or appeasement. As is common in the black vernacular at *this time*, "I am keeping it 100." I posit that one of our major societal problems regarding *race* is that many black people oftentimes minimize the impact of their race-related experiences and their feelings when relating those occurrences and emotions to sympathetic white people—who seem receptive and concerned—so as not to alienate them. This minimization of the impact results in a sugar coating of a bitter pill. Those who swallow the sugar-coated pill never get a true appreciation for the bitterness that lies at its core.

For my white brothers and sisters, as you read *my* memoir, I expect that many of you will argue regarding certain points that I make in the book. As a university-trained critical thinker and critical writer, most of my claims are warranted by my presentation of evidence. Even though this writing is a memoir, I strove to keep my claims and assertions on a scholarly level. I ask that the reader (1) keep an open mind, and (2) walk in my shoes—place yourself in my place—in instances with which you take issue.

I have a two-fold purpose in writing this book: (1) To tell the story and the experiences of The First Five and (2) to honestly discuss race as one with great experience with and grave concern for race relations in this country. I present, in cathartic fashion, the feelings, emotions, and hurts attendant to my early experiences. Contemporaneously with my cathartic expressions and the laying down of facts about The First Five, I provide reflexive comments on race and its absurdity as a foundation for human relations, particularly in these *United* States.

My University of Alabama sports experiences did not occur in a vacuum, but they occurred in the broader University educational and societal contexts of the times. Observe that when I enrolled at the University of Alabama in the fall of 1966, only three years had passed since then Governor George C. Wallace made his infamous "school house door" stand to block the enrollment of black students Vivian Malone and James Hood. As I recall it, there were only 43 blacks enrolled as I began my freshman year. Some sources say that there were 300 blacks enrolled at that time; however, experientially I know that 43 is a more accurate number. Probably all of the Bama black students who were enrolled that year would laugh at the "300" estimate; there were so few of us that we all knew each other or at least—about each other.

For high clarity as I present my experiences related to race at the University of Alabama, *overt* hatred and racism were not constantly on full display, but *silent* expressions of hatred shone through more subtly in mannerisms and practices, which hung in the atmosphere like a heavy ubiquitous fog. My experience is that hate and racism need not manifest in obvious overt ways to be real or hurtful.

I submit that the pervasiveness of subsurface hatred and racism can be just as injurious as overt surface hatred and racism. I view hatred and racism as a two-edged sword, which injures the hated as well as the hater. On December 7, 1964, in a speech in London, England, on segregation, Dr. Martin Luther King, Jr. put it this way: "Segregation injures the soul or the mind of the segregated as well as the segregator. It gives the segregator a false sense of superiority, while leaving the segregated with a false sense of inferiority."

ACKNOWLEDGMENTS

First of *all*, I thank God for keeping me safe during those early days of segregation and desegregation at the University of Alabama. I had no thought of the dangers and the kind of treatment that lay ahead—I was only 18 and unwise to the ways of the world that I lived in; "fools rush in where angels fear to tread." I went in and I came out unscathed—physically.

Without the financial sacrifices of my father, Leslie Pernell, and my mother, Mary Pernell, I most likely would not have been able to attend the University of Alabama. Posthumously, I thank both of them for their love and support throughout their lives.

This book has been in the works for several years. My wife, Chelsea T. Pernell, continuously prodded me to finish my book. Oftentimes she would chide me publicly in church for my spirit of procrastination. She allowed me periods of time off from our business and allowed me quiet time so that I could finish this work that has been shut up in my bones for a long time.

I would be remiss if I did not thank Prof. John David Briley, who provided—through his book—the impetus for me to tell *my* story in this memoir. Although my assessment of Coach Paul "Bear" Bryant differs with his regarding the efforts of the coach to integrate, I owe a huge "Thank you" to him for not forgetting about The First Five. The accuracy of his reporting about me during those earlier years was quite uncanny even though he had not been able to contact me over the years to get my input.

To reporter C. J. Schexneyder, I also owe a debt of gratitude for providing me with materials from those early days that captured the times in which The First Five made their debut. C. J. also wrote articles in which he recognized—probably more than many—the real significance of the acts of The First Five. Thank you, sir.

To my three strong sons, Brian Andre Pernell, Leland Christopher Wilson, and Brian Christopher Pernell, I leave this book and its contents as part autobiographical in ways that give you a glimpse into who your introspective dad is/was and as part of my commission to you to *stand* (or kneel) as circumstances require. To whom much is given, much is expected.

CHAPTER 1

Who, Exactly, Is White?

In an article that appeared in *The Undefeated* in its February 10, 2017 issue, writer Brando Simeo Starkey titled his article, *White Immigrants Weren't Always Considered White—and Acceptable*. Starkey wrote this:

> "Who, exactly, is white? The answer sounds obvious—we know a white person when we see one, we think. But when Italians poured into America in the late 1880s and early 1900s, they were not considered white upon arrival. The story of how European immigrants during that era became white

enlightens us on our current political realities. Italians, Greeks, Poles, Hungarians, Slavs and other European groups, at the time called 'new immigrants,' sought to overcome their subordination by showing, through their behavior, to be deserving of being considered white."

I would add that these new immigrants no doubt had to show their disdain for blacks in an exaggerated fashion such that *established* white folks could see that the new immigrants were just like them in their behavior and attitudes toward blacks. This statement reminds me of a statement made by the late comedian Richard Pryor during the days when blacks were first being accepted on police forces. Paraphrasing, he said that a black cop had to whip a black person's head worse than a white cop would in order for the black cop to show the white cop that he was one of them.

Starkey continued:

In 1911, Henry Pratt Fairchild, an influential American sociologist, said about new immigrants,

"If he proves himself a man, and…acquires wealth and cleans himself up—very well, we might receive him in a generation or two. But at present he is far beneath us, and the burden of proof rests with him. They ultimately met that burden and crucial to their success was that they were not black and they actively helped in maintaining a racist society."

Starkey continued with his comments, which were informed by a book by historian David R. Roediger, *Working Toward Whiteness*. Roediger's book explained how new immigrants became white: "Between 1886 and 1925, 13 million new immigrants came from southern, eastern and central Europe. Up until that point, people considered white generally hailed from England, the Netherlands, Ireland, Germany and Scandinavian countries." Roediger, a professor at the University of Illinois, argues that new immigrants, until they were fully brought into the white family, lived in a state of "in-betweenness," meaning they were placed in a racial pecking order below whites but above people of color.

Greeks, for example, fretted about being mistaken for Puerto Ricans, mulattoes or Mexicans. J. D. Ross, an Alabama politician, dubbed himself the "white man's candidate" and campaigned on Greek disenfranchisement. In Utah, Greek and Italian copper miners were classified as "non-white." White workers in Steelton, Pennsylvania, refused to take "hunky jobs"—jobs traditionally held by Hungarians—even during the poor economy of 1908, preferring unemployment. Isn't that funny?

Remember Jimmy the Greek? He was a sports commentator and bookmaker. He was fired from his job at CBS after giving an interview in January 1988, in which he said that black athletes are better than white athletes because the blacks have been "bred" that way. Aside from this remark, he said some very complimentary things about the prowess of black athletes; however, he used the term "bred."

Usually we think of "bred" as a term used in reference to animals and breeds of animals. Given the atrocious history of America with the construct of slavery and how the white man handled his property, such a term was not only politically incorrect, it was very *telling* as to the speaker's mindset. How does one come to be bred? Who controls the breeding? The conjuring up of those mental pictures should be very distasteful to all humans.

Remember Al Campanis—a Greek—former general manager and vice president of the Brooklyn Dodgers baseball organization who lost his job because of racial comments he made during a *Night Line* interview with Ted Koppel on April 6, 1987? Responding to a question by Mr. Koppel as to why there weren't any black managers, black general managers, or black owners in major league baseball, Mr. Campanis began by explaining that the reason was that in baseball you have to pay your dues and that the minor league jobs were low paying jobs. Mr. Koppel cut him off by saying that Campanis' explanation was "baloney." Campanis continued by explaining that blacks didn't have the mental "necessities" to be in management positions. He said that for that very reason, you don't have black NFL quarterbacks or black pitchers in major league baseball.

Speaking of Greeks and immigrants, Jimmy the Greek Anglicized his name; his birth name was Dimetrios Georgios Synodinos; he changed his name to "James George Snyder." Jimmy no doubt knew—or his parents no doubt knew—that Jimmy would have it easier in life without the Greek baggage. I am sure he didn't want to experience life here in America as a "non-white." Al Campanis' given name was Alexander Sebastian Campanis. Was "Al Campanis" less ethnic than "Alexander Sebastian Campanis?"

Isn't it funny how quickly some people forget that they and their ancestors were not always considered "white," but were once *classified* as "non-white"? Did they even *know* their history in this country? Knowing their racial status in this country should have made them more empathetic with the circumstances and treatment of black people and not so quick to ascribe negative traits to other non-white people.

I remember a comment that a white high school "friend" of my wife made. He is from Dublin, Georgia. He posted a picture of President Obama on the tailgate of his pick-up truck, with the inscription: "Does my ass look big to you?" The pick-up truck was a clue as to who he was.

What does it take to be recognized as a certified *racist?* I urged my wife to call her so-called friend and confront him with his cute little saying. He emphatically stated, "I'm not a racist, *though.*" In this paragraph, I had written a list of 10 telltale signs that one is a racist. I grappled with the thought of including the list in this book. After *weeks* of consideration, I thought that the best course was not to include them here. I did not want to establish a profile—a stereotype—lest some people be included who shouldn't be and others be excluded who should be included.

I will say this: If I did create such a racist profile—a good predictive one—individuals could assess their own racism index by the number of qualifiers that applied to them specifically; moreover, neither one of these telltale signs would be definitive when considered in isolation; however, when the telltale signs are compounded, a clearer picture develops. With the advent of Donald Trump, the traditional telltale signs are not as useful anymore for identification purposes; this is evident in the *broad* demographics of those who voted for Trump.

Al Campanis met only one of the unlisted telltale signs—he was "white." Al Campanis was an immigrant, though; he was born to Greek-speaking parents in Kos, a small Dodecanese Greek island in the Aegean Sea. He came to this country when he was six. Somehow, somewhere along his way, he had *learned* the notion that black people were inferior to white people. Not only did he learn and embrace this notion, he believed it enough to spew it on national television.

Had Campanis interacted with a statistically significant sample of both black and white people to make his "mental necessities" claim or had he been merely exposed to white folks who had conducted themselves as though this statement was true? Greek people were not even considered white for a long time. Even Campanis' whiteness—which I am sure he identified with—is in question. Is that not ironic? Note that racism is not limited to one's actions, but also applies to one's thoughts and attitudes.

Operational Definition: White Folks vs. White People

In this book, I will be talking at length about *white* folks and *white* people. I make an operational distinction because my intent here is not to indict an entire race, as white society is prone to do with certain negative occurrences involving some or even just one black person. For example, when news reporters broadcast that a person committed a crime without first revealing the race of the perpetrator, we, as black people wait with bated breath—hoping that the perpetrator is not black. We know experientially that white society has a propensity for ascribing individual abhorrent behavior by one or a few blacks to the entire black race in general. My point is that we are a proud race and like all other races, we have the good, the bad, and the ugly, but we wish not that dispersion be cast upon the whole race for the acts of a few.

When a white person commits a crime, black people do not routinely indict the white race for the sins of one or a few. For high clarity, I believe that there are good and bad people in *every* race and that anyone *can be* racist; however, I submit that racism in the hands of the powerful is much more dangerous and injurious. In regards to racism, this book discusses racism in terms of white *folks* and white *people* and their relationship to and with black people. The term "white folks" will characterize members of the Caucasian race who root *against* black people at every turn simply or mainly because of the latter's race. The term "white people" will refer to members of the Caucasian race who are empathetic and sympathetic to and supportive of equality, fair play, "and justice for *all*."

As Dr. Martin Luther King, Jr. said in one of his speeches, "There are some *white people* who are as determined as we are to see us free." I pause to acknowledge the life-giving civil rights work done in the early days by heroic and martyred white civil rights workers Viola Liuzzo, Andrew Goodman, and Michael Schwerner—all of whom paid the ultimate price.

Mrs. Liuzzo was a 39-year-old white civil rights activist from Detroit, Michigan, and the mother of five. She was shot twice in the head by members of the Klu Klux Klan on March 25, 1965, after the Selma to Montgomery March, while working on the "Freedom Summer" campaign trying to register blacks to vote. Schwerner, 24, and Goodman, 20, both white—were working alongside black freedom fighter James Chaney, 21, when they were all shot at close range and killed by members of the Mississippi White Knights of the Klu Klux Klan in Neshoba County, Mississippi, on June 21, 1964. As I conducted my research on these three *human beings*, I am amazed once again at man's inhumanity to man.

How could white folks be so cruel—not just to black people, but also to those white people who both sympathized and empathized with blacks? At some point in our history, the erroneous notion took hold that whites were *so superior* to black people that whites could not deal with blacks as human beings or those who supported blacks. God created all of us. As a Christian, I suggest to you that God is not pleased at how white folks have treated His creation.

If It Walks Like a Duck...

In 2019, black quarterbacks are so prevalent that mentioning that fact is no longer noteworthy. Campanis followed his comments with, "I'm not a racist";

he explained that a couple of b

And? U. S. Attorney General Je

behalf during his confirmation he

at this writing Jeff Sessions' prolifi

for an Alabama senate seat.

Guess what? The race is close i

Trump supported candidate, Tommy Tu

and football coach, coached many black

closeness to black players seem to have h

leanings. Isn't that funny?

Speaking of Jeff Sessions, I have observ ...ks

have a Negro or two that they take a liking to ...n far above

the rest of us and treat them almost as if they w ...c. Remember movie

director Quentin Tarantino's 2012 film *"Django"* and the slave antagonist

"Stephen," played by Samuel L. Jackson? Stephen, although he was a slave,

he was much harder on the other slaves than the white master. Stephen was

favored and trusted by the white slave master to keep the other slaves in

line. Stephen relished his job; his mannerisms and disposition were that of

a white overseer.

CHAPTER 2

Born into Segregation

I was born on January 19, 1948, in the *basement* of Bessemer General Hospital in Bessemer, Alabama—about 12 miles from historic Birmingham, a.k.a, "Bombingham." Yes, I said "basement"—that's where the Negro children and their parents were assigned. During visits to the hospital years later, I observed the exposed water pipes and sewage pipes running across the ceiling of the basement in the hospital rooms where black people were housed. The South has such an ugly history, filled to the brim with such incidents as this and much worse. As much as some would like to forget such things, they *did* occur.

As I reflect on the circumstances of my birth and that of other black babies born during that time, I understand that the basement relegation was a metaphor for the future life of many black children and black people. Entrance into the world for black people was at the literal bottom. The existing strict segregationist laws made the remainder of life's journey an uphill climb for black people. Relegating black people to disadvantageous situations placed white people in advantageous situations—wasn't that the plan from the beginning?

I remember Dr. Terry's medical office in Bessemer. When I was growing up, we would visit the doctor's office periodically. There was one waiting room for whites and a separate waiting room for coloreds—how thoughtful—we had some place to go to receive medical attention. We never saw the white patients on the other side of the wall. I wonder, in what *order* did Dr. Terry wait on his patients?

My Family Background

I was the youngest of three children. My older brother and sister were offsprings of my mother's previous marriage. Their dad was killed in a hunting accident when my brother was two years old and my sister was just six weeks old. There was never any "step-child" drama in our house—my brother and sister were my *brother* and *sister*—period. My dad was their dad.

The world in which I lived when I was growing up in the 50s and 60s was completely segregated. I was considered a smart kid in school; I was always near the top of my class in each grade—school work was easy for me—except algebra and some math related subjects; however I loved geometry and trigonometry. Being always conscientious about my scholastic work, I never had to explain bad grades to my parents.

My father and mother were good providers for their family. For most of my father's adult life, he was a coal miner, which caused him to develop—after 38 years in the coal mines—Black Lung disease in later life. My mother was a *domestic*—a euphemism for custodian of white folks' homes. Neither my father nor my mother completed or even attended high school, but they were both intelligent. Both of my parents worked without experiencing any long periods of unemployment. I discovered years later that we were poor; however, we didn't view ourselves as *poor* at the time. We always had enough to eat and we had a car. It seemed that just about everyone in my neighborhood had attained the same level of economic "success"—minus the car.

It appears that when *born into* a particular economic class, one adjusts rather easily to that class and it becomes a *natural* way of life. An analogy can be drawn with being born into a racist family or community or society. One's racist actions and attitudes become *natural*, without much *thought* or questioning of the correctness or hurtfulness of one's actions and attitudes; however, as natural as such actions and thoughts may be, they do not necessarily equate with right and justice. There *has to be* something that trumps environmental influences and norms and mores. I submit that there *is* something in us that is innate that informs us of what is right and what is wrong; however, I further submit that cultural norms and traditions oftentimes win out when courage is absent.

Coming of Age in Alabama in the '50s and '60s

I am now a 72-year-old African-American man. I lived in segregated Alabama for the first 22 years of my life, with the exception of my junior year in high school when I lived in Akron, Ohio. Until my junior year, contact with whites was limited to the occasions when I went downtown (Bessemer, Alabama) shopping or when the white insurance agent, a.k.a., *policy man*—came to my house weekly to collect the insurance premiums. Growing up, I remember the policy man always addressed my mother and father by their first name; one day when I was home from college, I sternly educated the policy man about the dangers of calling my mother by her first name and not putting the "Mrs." handle on her name. I never saw him again.

As I reflect on the policy man, I recall that *all* white people addressed all black people by their first name—no matter the age of the black person or the age of the white person. I remember little white children who my mother babysat, addressing her as "Mary." That's the way it was—no respect.

As I share this paragraph, a thought came to mind: Maybe if whites addressed black folks by their last name, it might be embarrassing to some whites in the community who share their same last name. Think about it. If the policy man addressed my mother as "Mrs. Pernell," and there was a white Mrs. Pernell, well, you can see how that could be a little embarrassing. For the uninformed, that means that the white Pernells may have owned the black Pernells—wouldn't that be funny?

Overcrowded Schools

The name of the elementary school that I attended was "Robertstown Negro Elementary School." Overcrowded classrooms were a fact of life during my elementary school years. I attended school only four hours a day—either 8:00 A.M. – 12:00 noon or 12:00 noon – 4:00 P.M. as part of the white folks scheme to deal with overcrowding in black schools. I must admit that many years later, makeshift trailers were installed at *some* of the black schools to deal with overcrowding—how ingenuous.

As a child, I thought that these double sessions were great! Double sessions allowed us to have *more play time*. Double sessions for me ended with the advent of my seventh grade year; however, there were 69 other students in my seventh grade class and just one teacher. Before class began each day, we were lined-up outside facing the flag and the big black and white sign that proclaimed, "Robertstown Negro Elementary School." We pledged "allegiance to the flag of the United States of America and to the republic for which it stands, one nation, under God, indivisible, with liberty and justice for all." How about that for indoctrination and hypocrisy?

At the time, we were blissfully ignorant to the fact—and our teachers too—that we were buying into this big lie. I observe that white folks become irate when a black person does not rise to pay *respect* to the flag when the Star

Spangled Banner is played; they want black people to accept the symbolism but not bother with the reality. This happened to me recently (2019) when I was at my son's football game and I did not stand for the national anthem. At the end of the anthem, a white guy yelled out, "U.S.A." He must have thought that he was still at a Trump rally. I know that the comment was aimed at me. I should have addressed him, but there were witnesses.

The *St. Petersburg Times* (April 13, 1967) provided this quote from a university official: "The Negro secondary schools are so poor that when it comes to doing college work the Negro student doesn't stand much of a chance." I wondered if the university official ever considered *how* the Negro secondary schools became so poor. The system had been rigged from the outset to produce inferior education for black children—overcrowding, poor facilities and equipment, and substandard teaching materials. This segregation device is a cleverly, devilishly designed system that feeds on and perpetuates itself so that at the end of the day people can justify their decisions with, "See, they are not intelligent enough to compete with our kids, otherwise we would have recruited them to play for us" or "that's why we don't hire them—very disingenuous and evil!

Separate and Unequal

I have been aware of race from at least the age of ten years old. Around that time, I wrote an essay in fifth grade that dealt with the economic ridiculousness of having separate water fountains, separate restrooms, separate lunch counters, separate theaters for blacks and whites, and this list goes on and on. I guess that was the businessman in me at an early age—or maybe it was a strong yearning for justice in me even in my formative years. Blacks and whites were kept apart or kept themselves apart as much as possible.

Segregated schools were the order of the day. In high school, I attended segregated Brighton High School. Brighton High School was located about five miles away from Bessemer in the city of Brighton. I shouldn't even have to say "segregated Brighton High School; *everything* was segregated. There was a Bessemer High School in *my* hometown of Bessemer, but that high school was reserved for white students; so, I was *bussed* to *another* city—

Brighton—to attend high school where there was a black high school. As I pen this, it all seems so ridiculous to me—how about you? Why did it have to be that way? Why?

I remember that back in that day, white folks vehemently complained about bussing; they didn't want *their* kids to be bussed, i.e., use a bus as a means of transportation to school. My thought at the time was that kids enjoy riding the bus. My wife and I owned several child care centers where we bused children to and from school. I could see the kids' excitement each time they boarded the bus. Someone commented at the time, "It ain't the bus, it's us."

With the exception of my junior year, I spent my high school years at Brighton High School. By the way, I was a third string and second-string quarterback during my freshman and sophomore years, respectively. I neglected to inform my coach that I would not be attending Brighton High for my junior year; when I returned for my senior year, my coach *let me know* that he had big plans for me for my junior year. Even though I did not play football my junior year while I was in Ohio, I did return to Brighton and lead my team to the Jefferson County Championship game.

The Northern Challenge

The word on the street in my circles was that the students in the "North" were smarter than the students in the South. I have a quiet, but very competitive nature and I wanted to see personally if there was any truth to this rumor. I had not mentioned to anyone the reason that I wanted to prove this adage wrong. My sister, who is about eight years older than me, lived in Akron, Ohio, and she allowed me to come and live with her and her family for that period of time.

I performed my best academically; with the exception of Algebra II, I was almost a straight A student. I placed ninth in English and second in French on the Ohio District-State Scholarship Test. Isn't it funny how I forsook football to go and disprove an academic rumor? Well, I didn't actually forsake football to prove a point. I tried out for the team and made it, but I quit shortly before the season began because the coach made it known early on that he had already identified, based on the previous season, key players for particular positions and quarterback was one of them.

I felt that I wasn't being given a fair chance. That was the first time that I ever quit anything. Later, I regretted quitting because the first string quarterback was injured in the first or second game of the season and was out for the year. If I had not quit, I probably would have received significant playing time. I learned a lesson for life: Never quit. Quitting eliminates *all* chances of winning or succeeding.

I must add that even though I was away from home, I continued to attend school every day. Toward the end of my junior year, 1965, my homeroom teacher began passing out Perfect Attendance certificates. I had received about seven or eight Perfect Attendance certificates over the years. I inquired of my teacher why I did not receive a Perfect Attendance certificate—I had never been absent. My teacher informed me that I missed *half* of a school day on a certain day during the school year.

The half-day that I missed was when I requested and received an excused absence for the afternoon. This was the day that there was a civil rights march or event in Akron and I attended. I wondered, was this action by my teacher the rule or was it retribution?

Old Film Footage of Man's Inhumanity to Man

Recently, I watched some archived footage from the 1960s of desegregation efforts and accompanying protests in several Southern cities. Sometimes when I watch old film footage of white folks protesting or rioting to show their undignified support for race separation in almost every aspect of life, I wonder, where are they now? What are they doing? Do they have black friends or neighbors or bosses? Are they members of the Klan or Tea Party or just plain old right wingers or, are they now hiding behind the euphemistic "conservative" tag? Have they adjusted well to the changed society in which they now live or are they placing their hope in Trump that he will "Make America Great Again?" Not that I care—just curious.

The sheets and the hoods are artifacts of a bygone era, but we know them now by their "red state-ness" and all that that entails in regards to racial inequality. What bolds ill for black people *and* America is that there are more red states than blue states, but thank God that Trump did not win the *popular vote*—there is hope!

Where are the white Birmingham firemen who turned their hoses on men, women and children—pinning them against buildings? Where is the white Birmingham policeman in the infamous photo that shows him holding a black student protester while he sics his dog on the student protester? Where are the Selma State Troopers who rode their *horses* into the crowd on the Edmund Pettus Bridge and tear gassed and beat the marchers on Bloody Sunday on March 7, 1965? Where are the white folks who cheered their actions?

Note that these violent white, domestic terrorists were acting under the auspices of their local or state government—government-sanctioned terrorism. By their mannerisms and facial expressions, it is obvious that they performed their "jobs" with a fierce passion—they were being true to their inner man. These domestic terrorists, in one form or another, swore to protect and serve. We see how that worked out.

Exposure

I sincerely wish that there was a way to identify these *white folks* and those like them so that they can get the *public* recognition that they deserve for their atrocious, dastardly deeds. I hate when they "throw a rock and hide their hand"—or dawn a sheet and hood to hide their face. I wish that these white folks could not blend in with the *white people*. I like to know whose who; this way, I *know* who's friend and who's foe. By being able to blend in or hide behind white people, the white folks enjoy an undeserved persona of decency and civility by hiding under the coat tails of white people.

I wanted to publish old photos—and later ones too—with names attached, catching them in action spewing racist venom; however, time constraints did not permit the required research. Many of us have seen the police dogs attacking black marchers in Birmingham, Alabama, in 1963. The vicious dogs were not attacking on their own volition; they were under the control of white policemen. The white folks in the mobs at Central High School in Little Rock, Arkansas, in 1954—I can see their hateful scowls even now—their filthy mouths exploding with ungodly words of hatred, detestation, and scorn.

The goal of public recognition and exposure was to leave a record for the progeny of these white folks so that their descendants will know their family history regarding race and where their parents and grandparents stood in relation to justice and fair play for all. Maybe and hopefully the threat of such exposure would encourage white folks to be more thoughtful in their speech and behavior—wishful thinking? After the publicized senate impeachment farce of Donald John Trump, with Republican senators burying their heads in the sand, I have no more disillusionment that exposure would be beneficial to changing behaviors.

CHAPTER 3

The Milieu of the Times

To provide context for my University of Alabama experience, which began in the fall of 1966, I share with you some notable events that hopefully will provide the historical backdrop and convey the *tone* and *climate* of the times: In 1896 in Plessy v. Ferguson, the court allowed segregation in schools; 58 years later in Brown v. Board of Education of Topeka (1954), Justice Earl Warren's court voted 9-0 in its decision that said that "...separate educational facilities are inherently unequal."

Two years prior to the ruling in Brown v. Board of Education of Topeka, Autherine Lucy became the first black to enroll at the University of Alabama; however, after University administrators discovered her race, they denied her admittance. Two years after the landmark court decision of 1954, Ms. Lucy re-enrolled (1956); however, mob violence ensued and the University expelled her after only two days of classes under the guise of protecting her. After researching Ms. Lucy's horrific experience with the University of Alabama, tears began to well up in my eyes as I read in detail about the brutal inhumane treatment that she received in her attempt to obtain an education at the University of Alabama.

Just recently, I learned that Ms. Lucy-Foster had returned to the Tuscaloosa campus in 1988 and graduated with a Master's Degree. More recently, she received an honorary doctorate degree from the University of Alabama. Furthermore, she has a tower on campus named in her honor: "The Autherine Lucy Tower." Excellent and sincere gestures, but why does it take so long to say, "I am sorry" and get it right?

Seven years after the 1956 enrollment of Autherine Lucy, Vivian Malone and James Hood attempted to enroll at the University of Alabama in 1963. As they attempted to enter Foster Auditorium to register for classes, segregationist Governor George C. Wallace blocked the entryway. After some persuasion by United States Deputy Attorney General, Nicholas Katzenbach, Wallace stepped aside.

There were some bombings subsequent to and related to their enrollment, but these two students were undeterred. Similar to Autherine Lucy, Vivian Malone and James Hood now have a plaza named in their honor on campus: "The Vivian Malone and James Hood Plaza." In 2000, Vivian Malone gave the commencement address at the University of Alabama. Again, why does it take so long to do right and get it right?

Lee v. Macon County Board of Education (1963) was a pivotal case in the integration of public schools in Alabama. Even though Brown v. Board of Education of Topeka (1954) had been decided that desegregation would be the law of the land regarding public education, Alabama and its chief agent, Gov. Wallace, fought integration at every turn. The initial defendant in the law suit was an all-white Tuskegee High School (in Macon County); however, the law suit was subsequently expanded to include all of the state's primary schools, secondary schools, two-year colleges, and public universities. A three-judge federal district court, in March 1967, ordered all of the state's public schools desegregated.

On August 27, 1963, the March on Washington was convened in which civil rights leaders called for civil rights and economic rights. About 250,000 civil rights leaders and groups united to show their resolve for civil rights and justice. On the following day, Dr. Martin Luther King, Jr. delivered his now famous, "I Have a Dream" speech in which he decried racism and injustice.

On September 15, 1963, the 16th Street Baptist Church in Birmingham was bombed, resulting in the death of four little black girls—a "Christian Nation"?—I don't think so. I was at my own church that sad Sunday morning; when I returned home, I heard the dreadful news. I was both sad and mad—feeling helpless.

The church had been the rallying place and training ground for civil rights activities. One week prior to the bombing, Alabama Governor George C.

Wallace had stated in the *New York Times* that in order to stop integration, what was needed was a "few first class funerals."

A few months earlier, on June 11, 1963, Governor Wallace made his infamous "School House Door" stand at Foster Auditorium at the University of Alabama Tuscaloosa campus. Wallace declared, "Segregation now, segregation tomorrow, segregation forever." This stand was in keeping with his campaign pledge.

No doubt the white citizenry *supported* Wallace to the point where he was willing to make this infamous stand; otherwise, Wallace would not have declared it—right? He was a politician and a racist; he gave the white folks what they wanted. Just three years later, I successfully registered for the freshmen class at Foster Auditorium.

On July 2, 1964, the Civil Rights Act was enacted which outlawed unequal application of voter registration requirements, addressed racial segregation in schools and public accommodations. On August 6, 1965, the Voting Rights Act was signed into law by then President Lyndon Johnson, which allowed African-Americans to *freely* register to vote; heretofore, African-Americans had been denied the right to vote by the employment of various mean-spirited strategies in Southern states—including physical violence. It is clear that voter suppression efforts are once again being implemented in not so cleverly guises across the country.

The most infamous and blatant assault on the 1965 Voting Rights Act was a decision that was handed down by the United States Supreme Court in Shelby County v. Holder (2013). The court struck down Section 4 of the Voting Rights Act. This section of the act required pre-clearance for states with histories of discrimination in their voting practices. The striking down of Section 4 also effectively neutered Section 5, which required voting changes in the identified states be subject to an administrative review or court review for the purpose of showing that the changes were neither discriminatory nor had the effect of being discriminatory. It is noteworthy that the court ruled 5-4 in Shelby County v. Holder.

Since April, 2020, the *United States Supreme Court* has voted four times, each by 5-4 (five Republicans, four Democrats) margins, to effectively disenfranchise voters. This disenfranchisement, I would argue, was mainly to suppress the black vote and the Latino vote. Some of the tools of voter suppression that are being employed currently are (1) gerrymandering, (2) intimidation, (3) elimination of early voting and Sunday voting, (4) drastically reducing the number of polling places, (5) requiring various and sundry forms of identification, (6) fighting against mail-in voting, and (7) removing voters from the voting rolls—to name a *few*.

The good white folks of Alabama were so repulsed by the Civil Rights Act of 1964 and the Voting Rights Act of 1965 that President Johnson, a Democratic, signed into law that they hurriedly changed their political party affiliation to the Republican Party—which was much more aligned with their way of life and their level of comfort. Circa 1968, then President Nixon, implemented his Southern Strategy to consolidate the white Southern voters in order for the Republican Party to win presidential elections. The Southern Strategy, scholars agree, involved *racial backlash* at the Democrats for inviting black people into the tent.

Since the events cited above are far removed from our consciousness and we have moved such a *great distance* away from those types of events, I thought it important to usher these happenings back into our remembrance of things past and for those who are too young to remember—an opportunity for enlightenment, awe, and expressions of shame. Oftentimes, we hear people "patting" themselves on the back about how far we've come in terms of race relations. I submit that even though we have come a ways, the patting seems to be premature.

The actions of The First Five were happening, not merely contemporaneously with, but tangentially to the cited foundational events above and share a continuity and kinship with those events. Highlighting these events here facilitates an appreciation of the (1) courage of The First Five, (2) the danger in which The First Five willingly and naively placed themselves, and (3) the significance of the actions of The First Five.

Marches, Demonstrations, and Sit-ins

During my senior year, 1965-1966, civil rights march organizers visited the local area black high schools in an effort to recruit students to leave school and travel to Birmingham (Alabama) to participate in civil rights marches and demonstrations. The principal at our school gave tacit approval to our leaving school by his inaction and silence. We were pleasantly surprised that our strict principal allowed such actions; maybe he realized that history was in the making. Many of the students left school during the school day, including me. We either got rides or caught busses to get to the 16th Street Baptist Church in Birmingham, which was the locus of the civil rights mass meetings and stagings of protest marches and demonstrations.

It was an extremely exciting time. We knew, at some level, that what we were doing was significant and right. We felt good about ourselves and what we represented. We were not at all fearful—we were naïve teenagers—placing ourselves in harm's way—not caring about or even considering the possible and probable consequences of our civil rights efforts. These were dangerous times; however, our naïveté combined with our courage, served as a catalyst for profound change in this country.

Once assembled inside the 16th Street Baptist Church, the march organizers would pump us up with stirring speeches and inspirational songs before we were led on various planned marches and protests. We enthusiastically sang inspirational songs like, "Which Side Are You on Boy," "Ain't Gonna Let Nobody Turn Us Around," and "We Shall Overcome." The lyrics and the beats are seared in my mind forever. Mass meetings were held at several area churches at night to keep the black populace informed and fired-up regarding the movement and its activities.

One night while my friends and I were walking back home to Bessemer from a mass meeting in Brighton, about five miles away, we saw the headlights of a line of cars that appeared to us as some type of procession. We immediately thought that these cars might contain members of the Klu Klux Klan and we dove into a roadside trench until the line of cars passed. It could have been just a line of cars, but such were the times.

In addition to my marching activities, mainly in Birmingham, I participated in local marches and demonstrations. I remember protesting in front of Velma's Café in Brighton because black patrons were required to walk through the ever-standing puddle of water to go to the *side door* to order and receive their food. One of my Dad's friends, Mr. Frank, saw me protesting in front of the restaurant and he told my Dad; I guess he was "telling on me." My Dad didn't say a word to me; by his silence, I knew that he approved. I guess that it was kind of like the silence from my high school principal when the march organizers came around; maybe they recognized that important long-needed change was afoot and they did not want to stifle it, albeit a dangerous undertaking.

Sit-In at McLellan's Department Store

One summer in 1963, while in high school, I organized a sit in at McLellan's in Bessemer. McLellan's was a department store with two lunch counters— one for whites and one for blacks too—how thoughtful. I now wonder if

McLellan's had devised a way to account for the revenues separately. I had eaten at the black lunch counter on many occasions; however, I had never even thought about eating at the white lunch counter, but one day I did think about it.

I was successful in recruiting three of my friends to go with me to sit-in at the white lunch counter at McLellan's five and dime store. Note that McLellan was gracious enough to provide two lunch counters—one for blacks and one for whites—in *different* sections of the store. The two separate lunch counters served dual purposes: (1) It kept the races separate—as was the custom *and* the law, and (2) it provided additional revenue to the store from the black lunch counter—the profit motive wouldn't let segregation stand in the way of revenue.

When we entered McLellan's, we found seats at the white lunch counter. Several whites were comfortably seated at the counter as we approached. All of the white patrons quickly vacated their seats at the counter. As soon as we sat down, the white cook advised us in a very agitated voice that, "Y'all don't belong here! Y'all eat over there!" I remember those words verbatim from over 50 years ago.

I remember one of the white men saying—as they stood behind us, somewhat taken aback by our audacity I guess—"They don't belong here; let's get 'em up." The same sentiments were expressed at the University of Alabama a few years later. We may not have been welcome, but we *did* belong here. They brought us over here—to provide free labor. We continued to sit for a while after we ordered—I ordered a strawberry shake and my friends placed their order—but we never received our orders. The white men did not attack us black teenagers; we had not contemplated what we would do if attacked.

As I penned this event, a quite poignant thought came to mind. Recently, our adult Sunday school lesson was entitled, "Counting the Cost of Discipleship" (Luke 14:25-35). In the lesson, Jesus advised his would-be disciples to count *all* of the costs associated with being a follower of Him. We young teenagers did not count the costs associated with our course of action. If we had, there was a good chance that we would not have staged a sit-in at the "Whites Only" lunch counter, or marched, or protested, or won our civil rights. I posit that the older generation had counted the costs—job, family, house, physical harm, etc.—and stayed on the sidelines. The younger generation was not encumbered with such *counting* and thereby moved boldly in the direction of a better America.

After a few minutes of no service, we got up and walked calmly and silently out the front door. As we were nearing the exit to the front of the store, two or three policemen passed us as they hurriedly walked in the direction of the lunch counter. We continued to exit calmly and silently. Once we got outside, we split up and ran out of downtown Bessemer as fast as we could go. We laughed about it later—that was so funny! Epilogue: A few years after the lunch counter incident, McLellan's closed its white lunch counter and left the remaining black lunch counter intact. Go figure.

The latest demographic figures for Bessemer reveal that the racial make-up of Bessemer is 70% black and 23% white. In 1960, the black population of Bessemer was just 43%. The City of Bessemer has had at least one black mayor since I was last a resident in 1984. Why do we have to go through all of this drama rather than do the right thing from the beginning? Why must the moral arc be so long?

The refrain, "Y'all don't belong here" is pregnant with the hatred that white folks had for blacks. When I went to the University of Alabama to register for my classes, the registrar in essence said, "Y'all don't belong here." When Governor George Wallace made his infamous school house door stand at Foster Auditorium at the University of Alabama, he was saying, "Y'all don't belong here." We understood that we were not welcome, but we also understood that *we did belong*!

Sit-Down in the Streets of Bessemer

On another occasion, I was participating in a sit-down in the streets of downtown Bessemer. I was sitting in the first row of demonstrators. The Bessemer fire department and the Bessemer police department were called out to disperse us. Shortly after we sat down in the street, the police waded into the crowd with their billy clubs. I remained seated, but when I looked back, I saw that the crowd had scattered—I joined them in their retreat.

During those turbulent times, the police and fire personnel served as agents and enforcers of the segregated social order. In elementary school when we received our second-hand textbooks, which had been previously used by white kids, we saw pictures of the police being friendly to the white citizenry. What was offered in the textbooks was not at all consistent with our experiences with the police. And, by the way, *all* of the people in our textbooks were white; the only character in our textbooks that was not white was Spot, the dog.

Years later—many years later—my son worked as a fireman and as a paramedic for the Bessemer Fire Department along with some other blacks. Of course, the fire department was lily white previously. By the time that my son and other blacks became a part of the Bessemer Fire Department, it had dispensed with its practice of hosing its black citizens. I wonder if hosing black citizens was a part of the training manual or something that the firemen just picked-up *naturally*.

Why is the South—Southerners—the very *last* to accept change—change that is right and just? That quality of reluctance to change lies at the heart of conservatism, which has no interest in justice and fair play for black people. Social *conservatism* and *racism* may not be synonymous, but for sure they are contrapositive to the welfare and well-being of a historically subjugated black people.

The Exodus and the Repatriation

I know both experientially and statistically that during the 60s, black high school graduates left Alabama en masse immediately after graduation from high school to find employment in more favorable "climates." I suspect that such high school and college graduates in other Southern states did likewise.

It is a shame that black high school graduates had to migrate to other "climates" in order to find suitable employment. This meant separation from families and other loved ones, as well as separation from their native *home*.

The period from 1941–1970 has been referred to as the "2nd Great Migration." Blacks moved to urban areas in the North and West to take jobs in thriving industries. By the close of this period, blacks had become urbanized; over 80% of blacks lived in cities.

Many of my contemporaries have returned to Alabama. Alabama is *home* to them; it is only natural that people would want to return home. Maybe they think it is safe to go home now—to enjoy the latter part of their life in relative peace and security. Although many have returned to Alabama, there are many more who are still living in the diaspora—separated from their Alabama homeland. Maybe this latter group feels as though they have been separated too long to return; maybe they have started families in their adopted states who have no connection with Alabama; maybe they have not forgiven Alabama and Alabamians for the treatment and conditions that forced them to adopt another home.

I can only imagine that white Alabamians feel a certain affinity for their state and other people from Alabama just by virtue of being Alabamians. I can only imagine that this affinity might express itself in this way: One University of Alabama graduate begins to conduct job interviews with college graduates from various universities from different states and among the interviewees is a graduate from the University of Alabama. I can only imagine how much weight that University of Alabama connection would carry in securing the job.

As support for my argument above, I present the words of Marion Jackson, a reporter for the *Birmingham World* newspaper (April 8, 1967) referring to Southeastern Conference schools:

> This pivotal concentration rivals in fermentation our quest for open occupancy, because true integration, equality, intellectualism and achievement cannot be realized under the separate but equal myth.
>
> Then too, the attitudes, challenge, friendships, esprit de corps, harmony which characterize college acquaintances and friendship and inter-class organizations and societies, have

persuasive influences on job, status, inter-group pursuits, and opportunities in everyday life.

Any alumnus of our academic halls of ivy will tell you that there is a carryover of campus acceptance into our work-a-day world and the permanency of such...is of solid rock. The granite truth of college forged idealism, the endurance and perseverance of campus ties, and the warm, glow of friendships, is a remarkable tool of our free enterprise system.

A case in point, my 17-year-old son and I visited a university in the Northeast a few months ago for an unofficial football visit. While one of the position coaches and I were talking, I mentioned my walk-on at Bama and he mentioned that he had played at Bama too—many years later—and we had a let-your-guard-down type of dialogue. After giving us a tour of the campus, the coach spoke encouraging words to my son such that my son was very hopeful of receiving a football scholarship. My son subsequently told me that he observed that the *Bama connection* was a difference maker. The encouragement from the coach was not offered in a vacuum; he had seen film of my son and he said that he was very impressed with my son's talent. As Alabamians, we should be looking out for each other no matter the difference in skin color.

CHAPTER 4

Welcome to the University of Alabama— My Transcript and the Registrar

I returned to Brighton High School for my senior year. I was a self-motivated student; it was not necessary for my parents to get on me about homework or grades or going to school every day. I loved school. I graduated fifth out of 212 classmates in my senior class; college was next on my horizon.

I received a four-year academic scholarship to Knoxville College in Knoxville, Tennessee, but I *wanted* to attend the University of Alabama. Wanting to attend Bama germinated in my subconscious. I liked challenges and I hated injustice. Attending the University of Alabama meant that my parents would have to foot the bill for my tuition, room and board, books, and fees. We were not a well-to-do family by any stretch of the financial imagination. I told my dad that I would rather attend Bama.

During those times, the man of the house made the financial decisions, I think that this was due to both tradition and the man was the chief, and sometimes, sole breadwinner. My father told me he would do what he could financially to help me and he did. My mother was in agreement. Without verbalizing it, I think my father *wanted* me to attend the University of Alabama—he also hated injustice. As I look back over my life, I have almost always taken "...the road less traveled by and that has made all the difference"

(Robert Frost, *The Road Not Taken*). Moreover, "A ship in harbor is safe—but that is not what ships are built for" (John A. Shedd).

During the spring of 1966, I applied to the University of Alabama for admission. The acceptance/enrollment process did not go smoothly. Early in the summer of 1966, after high school graduation, I received notice from the University of Alabama that the University had not yet received my transcript. My high school had documentation that my high school registrar sent my transcript to the University of Alabama in April of that year.

As I think about it today, I am very surprised that the University would even *notify* me—all things considered—the notification could probably have been a "clerical error." My thoughts regarding my notification germinated from my remembrance of reading that the University had mistakenly admitted Autherine Lucy in the first place—the University did not know that she was black. When the University discovered their "clerical error," the University expelled her.

I was in Detroit, Michigan, looking for summer work at the time that this notification was sent. I drove back home to Bessemer and my guidance counselor, Mr. Jefferson, and I—in response to this notification—drove from Bessemer to Tuscaloosa and hand-delivered my transcript to the University. Upon arrival, I was met by the University of Alabama registrar who informed me that my grades and test scores were not on a par with most of the other students and thus, recommended that I go somewhere else where I would be "happy"—*any place* but the University of Alabama I guess.

Needless to say, I didn't follow the registrar's recommended path to happiness for me. I wondered, as he considered my grades and test scores, had he factored in the *double sessions* and the *overcrowding* when I was in elementary school. I had been short-changed on my education for at least my first seven years of school. Now the registrar wanted to compare apples to apples, when his system intentionally created apples and oranges. Both apples and oranges can be successful; the oranges sometimes need a little consideration for the climate in which they were planted.

For the record, my grades and test scores met the entrance requirements, and I graduated in four years with a Bachelor's degree in Business Administration (Industrial Relations) from the University of Alabama. Subsequently, I graduated from Western International University in Phoenix,

Arizona, with a Master of Business Administration degree—carrying the tag of *magna cum laude*. In pursuit of a doctorate in Management at the University of Phoenix, my grade point average was 3.92—would have been a 4.0 but for that A- in philosophy. I am not enrolled in the doctoral program at this writing, but I will resume my doctoral quest soon after this book is published. I have had two professors volunteer to be on my dissertation committee because of my academic prowess—humph. Just imagine the possibilities if I had not been cheated out of my education in the *formative* years.

Freshmen Orientation

One memorable event occurred at Foster Auditorium at Freshmen Orientation. Remember, Foster Auditorium is the building where Gov. George Wallace "stood in the school house door" just three years earlier. A group of us black students were sitting *together* at a table completing the required registration forms. Since there was so few of us in this sea of white faces, we naturally gravitated toward each other. The auditorium was filled with other freshmen seated at rectangular-shaped tables completing their paperwork too. A black friend at our table named Danny needed a pencil and he asked one of the white freshmen guys at the table in front of us if he could borrow a pencil. The student said "No" even though he had in plain sight a *pack* of pencils.

The white student's hair was almost as curly as my hair; I guess he didn't want his heritage to be called into question by being kind to a black student. We black students laughed about the incident, but the laugh wasn't because the incident was funny. This is how we sometimes managed to handle these types of occurrences. White folks were just funny that way.

I remember an event in Bessemer, Alabama, that evoked similar laughs from my black friends. It was a centennial event celebration for Bessemer. Some of the Bessemer policemen—white of course—began beating some of the blacks who attended as if the policemen didn't want the blacks around; I think that this occurred during the 1960s. One of my teenage friends was hit in the temple area with a night stick. As we gathered the next day, we could clearly see the imprint from the carved nightstick on

Charlie's face; when we found out and saw this, we all laughed—but it wasn't a funny laugh. This is just how we managed to handle such occurrences—*sometimes*.

My White Roommate

My mother and father drove me down to the University in September of 1966 to begin my college career. We never discussed amongst ourselves what to expect and how to behave in this white environment. As I think about that now, I consider that strange. Maybe my parents didn't want to alarm me or maybe—they just did not have a clue as to what I was facing. There was never a mention of the novelty of my attending the University of Alabama. Back home in Bessemer, my father probably boasted among his crew, that he had a son in college and at *the* University of Alabama no less, but I am not sure.

As my mother waited in the car, my father and I carried my trunk up to my dorm room. When I opened the door, I could see that I had a white roommate—he was sitting at his desk with his back to the door—he never turned around. I guess he could tell that my father and I were black from the sound of our voices. There was no exchange of greetings or any other words between him and me as my father and I entered the dorm room.

My father and I dropped off my trunk and I went back downstairs to say goodbye to my parents. My father and I never spoke about the non-reception of my white roommate; as a matter of fact, we *never* talked about my experiences as a black student at the University of Alabama or as a football player—black men of my father's generation were into baseball—not football. When I walked back up to my room, my roommate was gone. Where did he go? Was it something that I said?

After a few minutes of unpacking my trunk, I decided to walk over to the campus store to pick up some toiletries and snacks. When I returned, I discovered that I didn't have a roommate anymore—he had moved out swiftly and *completely*. I can just imagine the haste with which he gathered all his belongings to be gone before I returned.

I really didn't give it a second thought at the time. I didn't even share with my parents what happened. I was really glad that I now had a "private" dorm room. I am more introverted than extroverted anyway, and I love my peace and solitude. As the Southern expression goes, "It was like throwing a rabbit in the briar patch."

Now that I think about that incident decades later—it had an impact. My white roommate sent me a clear message; he could not share a room with such an inferior person. That incident and a preponderance of like behavior have greatly influenced how I deal or interact with white folks, even now.

What would his friends think if they found out that he shared a room with a black student? I am sure that he would have lost his standing among his peers and may have been disowned by his family—really! I will say more about this when I discuss a locker room confession from a white player.

In spite of many reports of how *nicely* blacks were received by white students during these early years, these reports were more anecdotal in nature and were not representative of our broader reception or rejection. My white roommate's response was more indicative of the reception that we experienced as blacks on campus. I wonder where he is now and if he passed along this type of attitude and behavior to another generation.

A Few Among Many

Imagine being one of 43 black students among 10,000 white students in Alabama in the mid 1960's; we were less than one percent of the student body. I have seen figures of 300 black students enrolled at the time (1966). If this is true, I was certainly unaware of the other 257 black students. Even if the latter figure is right, we, blacks, were less than four percent of the student body.

The University of Alabama had an extension center in Birmingham referred to as the "Birmingham Extension Center of the University of Alabama at Birmingham." The center did not become autonomous until 1969 and was subsequently renamed "The University of Alabama at Birmingham (UAB). The only way to make the count of 300 blacks in 1966 would be to add the number of blacks enrolled at the extension center to that of the Tuscaloosa enrollment. During my four years at Bama, I remember having been the only black person in my class except for my freshman year algebra class and my senior year African American History class.

The Business Law Professor and the Students

I was sitting in the back of my Business Law class one sunny and warm Monday morning listening to the professor share, at the beginning of class, how his weekend had gone. He related, quite matter-of-factly, that over the weekend he had worked so hard in his yard pulling up weeds and cutting grass that there came a point where he "...was sweating like a *Nigger* on election day." The whole class laughed so hard; it must have been very funny; however, the humor escaped me. There was exactly zero consideration of my presence or my feelings. This was reminiscent of the times when "massa" would say anything around the house Negroes, no matter if the cruel language was concerning them or other blacks—as though they weren't there.

At the time, I knew that the professor's comment was very derogatory and racist. As I reflect on the comment now, I understand that there was more embedded in the comment. I have concluded that the professor and the students *knew* how hard and terrifying that white folks had made it for blacks to vote. White folks are funny that way; they have a knack of finding humor in our misfortunes. I think that part of this behavior is to soothe their conscious with jokes and laughter when the wrong is so egregious.

Remember the unjustified killing of Trayvon Martin by George Zimmerman? An acquaintance shared with me that she was in a store shopping in a predominantly white area in Cleveland, Ohio, and two white guys were talking, unaware that my acquaintance could hear them. She overheard one of them say, "Trayvon should have known better than to bring a pack of Skittles to a gun fight." The laughter stopped when the two white fellows discovered that she was within earshot and that she heard the comment. They *knew* that a wrong had been committed in the murder of Trayvon Martin; but for conscience sake, they tried to laugh away the atrocious act.

I learned an important lesson in one of my sociology classes that helped me not be so taken aback by comments like that of the prick who was my Business Law professor: One's level of professional and academic attainment and standing has little to do with one's attitude toward race or *changing* one's attitude toward race. The lesson taught me that the level of academic attainment and standing merely allows one to justify and express one's racist beliefs and actions more eloquently; however, the professor expressed his sentiments not so eloquently. I must hasten to add that this was the only professor who behaved in such a way towards me.

The Other Professors

I remember that after one grading period I received a "D" in an accounting course—I had a 68 average in the class based on several tests that I had taken. I had received an "A" on a pop quiz one Monday morning. I scored 108 out of a possible 110, but the instructor failed to factor this score into his grade for me. I figured that he had not counted my quiz score, so I sought him out in his dorm room—he was a student-teacher. I pleaded my case that certainly the 108 that I scored was worth at least two points. He finally agreed and he changed my grade to a "C" and I was glad about it.

Let me illustrate my starting point for learning introductory accounting: the course started with terms such as "debit" and "credit. I thought that I knew what "credit" meant; it was what you get when the business owner at the store sells you something and you don't have to pay for it immediately. Credit in the accounting sense was foreign to me, initially. Considering my starting point, a "C" in accounting was a major accomplishment for me. I struggled with my accounting course, but my struggle was successful. The registrar who attempted to steer me away from the University of Alabama probably didn't realize that I had *struggle* in me.

Several of my instructors were very encouraging. I remember that in my senior year, one of my instructors told the class that I ("Mr. Pernell") may be the only person in the class to easily find a job when I graduated. My major was Business Administration (Industrial Relations). I graduated in 1970 and the economy and job market were in the throes of a recession. My professor's name, the only one that I remember after 46 years, was Harold James. He was a "Northerner" and friendly towards me.

When I graduated and began looking for work, I found that my professor had misjudged my chances at gaining immediate employment. I remember applying at U.S. Steel in Fairfield, Alabama, for a job commensurate with my educational background. U.S. Steel was viewed as a choice place to work; many of my high school classmates had found employment there immediately after graduating from high school, but they were all blue collar-type workers—they worked in the plant—I wanted to work in the *office*.

The U.S. Steel job interviewer informed me that he would hire me but I would be given a clerical job and that there was no room for advancement. I now wonder why he shared with me that there would be "no room for advancement." That very same week, I boarded a Greyhound bus for Akron, Ohio, in pursuit of suitable employment. I applied to 43 different employers before I was finally hired—about four months after my graduation from Bama—making $400 a month—this was well below what I had anticipated making as a college graduate.

There was another business professor who complimented me on my negotiation skills. The class was given a group project; we were divided into groups of four or five. Each group represented a labor union and the professor represented management. Each group was given the task of obtaining concessions from management through negotiations.

My group, surprisingly, chose *me* to lead the negotiations. Our grade was dependent on how successful we were; if we, the union, went out on strike, we would receive a failing grade. Negotiating felt natural to me. I had pushed management to the brink, but in the end my team obtained the concessions we sought—without striking.

After the project was over for all groups, my professor informed the whole class that I was "the negotiator's negotiator." That one comment did wonders for my self-esteem and my self-worth. Those positive words spoken by my professor still provide confidence for me whenever I am involved in negotiations.

College Is Not a Social Experience

In an article in the *Crimson-White* student newspaper printed circa 1967, black student staff writer Bailey Thomson asked the question: "Where does a black man fit in socially in a predominantly white university?" Dean of Men, John L. Blackburn responded: "If a Negro student perceived college as a social experience, he should attend a Negro school," implying stereotypically that "Negro" schools were party centers—but not white schools.

Regarding Dean Blackburn's terse response, he should consider that the University of Alabama had a plethora of fraternities and sororities during that same time period. Today, the University of Alabama has approximately 67 fraternities and sororities. Katie Lambert writes about fraternities in her article, *How Fraternities Work*, and says: "Why would anyone want to join a fraternity? On the one hand, there's the promise of parties, living college life to the fullest, meeting pretty sorority girls and indulging in wild, alcohol-soaked adventures. On the other hand, there's the chance to become a leader and embody the values and ideals of a fraternity."

Do these revelations just fly in the face of Dean Blackburn's position on the "social experience"? I have *seen* the social experience at work at the University of Alabama (1966–1970). Talkin' 'bout a party! We were just not welcome to participate in the party.

Recently, while doing some research via the University of Alabama's website—many months after I had written this piece on Dean Blackburn, I came across a caption: Blackburn Institute; the "Blackburn" name popped out at me. My thought was, this is probably the same guy who made the disparaging remarks towards blacks and black universities that I reported in the above paragraphs.

At the Blackburn Institute (I took it to be), a photo showed a small racially mixed group standing in front of what appeared to be engraved marvel, with these words: "...until justice rolls down like waters, and righteousness like a mighty stream." I was immediately reminded of assistant football coach Mal Moore who went on to become the athletic director at the University of Alabama. Dean Blackburn, over a 30-year period, had risen to be a man of great standing at the University of Alabama. This is what the University of Alabama included in its bio of him: "He began his career at The University of Alabama in 1956 and he became Dean of Men in 1958. In 1963, his dedication to progress and meticulous planning were credited as key elements in the historic peaceful integration of African-Americans into the Capstone."

In Blackburn's 1967 warning to blacks, he recommended that blacks go to a black school if they think that they are going to come to the University of Alabama and party. Comparing Blackburn's previous statement about blacks' propensity to party with the recent bio comments regarding the giving of credit to Blackburn for his shrewd and thoughtful integration of African Americans into college life at the University of Alabama, should create cognitive dissonance in the reader. Maybe Blackburn's 1967 statement and what the University of Alabama said recently about his performance in 1963 are not necessarily at odds with each other; however, they *should* cause a *thinking* person to think more carefully about what they are hearing now. Blackburn's 1967 statement is part of the permanent record; but with the passage of time and memory, our remembrances seem to be as we want them—they make for a good story with a good ending.

CHAPTER 5

Social Awakenings

As I recall it, all of the surrounding male dorm students ate in one cafeteria, Paty Hall. Paty Hall was the newest of the area dorms. During meal times in the cafeteria, seating was hard to find because of the large number of students from the surrounding dorms coming to eat at about the same time at the same place. Almost without fail, if a black student was *lucky* enough to find a vacant seat at a table and he took the seat, the whole table of white students would become so outraged that *all* the white students would jump up as though they were on fire—I wish they had been on fire; they would either move to another table or take their tray to the conveyor belt and storm out of the cafeteria.

What was the big deal about sitting down to eat in close proximity to each other? Black kitchen workers had had their hands on and in their food throughout the preparation process. Now, when the food is put on the plate and on the table, a whole new set of rules comes into play. The *intimacy* that black kitchen workers have had with their food is not allowed to be transferred into intimacy in the consumption of the food in close proximity to black people. White folks are just funny that way.

Segregation is a contrived system of separation and for it to work, all parties to the system must play their roles as prescribed by the system. Wouldn't it make sense that if you are going to separate yourselves based on race and a false sense of superiority, the last thing that you would want is to have black people handling the food that goes into your body—right? Well, since it's convenient and saves you work, then OK. But they still have to show their sense of superiority by not consuming their meals alongside blacks. This was just a *rule* that did not and does not make any sense; it was a selfish rule; it was an illogical rule.

Some Anecdotes That Are both Relevant, Poignant, and Cause for Pause

I remember a real life story told by actor Sidney Poitier. Although Poitier was born in Miami when his family was visiting from the Bahamas, he grew up in the Bahamas and came to this country at the age of 16. He had not *learned* the mores, norms, and traditions associated with race in this country—at the time. He said that he got a job delivering packages to homes in the community.

Poitier shared that he knocked on the *front* door of this white woman's house to deliver a package to her. According to Poitier, she became so irate that he—a Negro—would have the audacity to come to her front door. After severely scolding him for failure to observe Southern protocol and failure to know his rightful place in the system of segregation and racial superiority, she ordered him to the proper place for a Negro to make deliveries to her home—around back.

Needless to say, Sidney Poitier went on to become a renowned movie star and director. In 1964, Poitier won an Academy Award for "Best Actor" in *Lilies of the Field*. In 2000, Poitier won the Screen Actors Guild "Lifetime Achievement Award." In 2001, he won the NAACPs Hall of Fame Award. In 2001 and 2009, he won Grammy Awards for "The Best Spoken Word Albums." This is the *same* Negro who was told to go to the back door.

Cleveland Browns Stadium

An incident happened at the Cleveland Browns Stadium that has stuck in my psyche. My wife and two of my sons had gone there at the invitation of a white woman who heard me give a speech at a private school regarding my University of Alabama experience. The Cleveland Browns were playing the Baltimore Ravens that particular night.

The woman, whose name I cannot recall, had connections to former University of Alabama football player extraordinaire, Ozzie Newsome.

Newsome was the general manager for the Baltimore Ravens at the time. The woman had arranged for Ozzie and I to meet at the game; she thought it would be a good idea, given my pioneering history at our alma mater; however, the meeting never took place because of some internal issues that were going on within the Ravens organization, she explained.

I was a bit disappointed and a bit more disappointed because Ozzie did not extend an invitation to meet at some other time and place. It seemed that our meeting was more desired by me and her than him. He was general manager of a pro football team and Hall of Fame inductee; I was just an obscure walk-on who hardly anybody knew. I still admire him though, as an outstanding football player and a man of great accomplishment.

The night of the Ravens and the Browns game, my wife and two of my three sons sat in our designated seats, next to a white couple who were already seated. Soon after we sat down, they got up and stood up near the railing; they never returned to their seats. Don't forget, this did not happen in Birmingham or Bessemer or Tuscaloosa, Alabama. This happened in Cleveland, Ohio. Is it just me or are white folks just funny that way? This is reminiscent of my Paty Hall cafeteria experiences at the University of Alabama 45 years ago.

I have only mentioned the incident once since it happened about four years ago; I mentioned it to my wife only recently. She, too, had observed and remembered the same incident; she too had never mentioned the occurrence. Isn't it odd that we did not comment on the incident to each other? What is it that makes us hold events like that inward? I had not talked about my First Five experiences to anyone, not even my wife, until almost 44 years later. It may be that we somehow become ashamed for the perpetrators and humanity in general and that we are sometimes reluctant to add to the heightening mountain of stories of man's egregious behavior toward his fellow man.

To call further attention to how experiences like these shape a person's psyche, my wife and I were in the Miami airport recently awaiting a flight back to Cleveland. I sat face-to-face across the aisle from a white woman, who was sitting comfortably and did not appear to be about to leave her seat. Two of my sons followed a few seconds later and sat next to me. The white woman immediately got up from her seat, never to be seen again. Did she move because we three blacks sat *near* her? I don't know. It could be just me, burdened with many memories of white folks getting up when I sat down near them.

Disrespect in the Miami Airport

My wife and I were sitting in the Miami airport in 2019, waiting for a flight back to Cleveland that was delayed several times. Passengers were becoming a bit frustrated with the periodic announcements that the flight would be even further delayed. A black woman passenger, I deduced from the sound of her voice, became "loud" with the ticket agent's lack of candor with particulars about the several delays.

My wife and I were seated in a row back-to-back with a white couple and other passengers. The guy's wife asked him, "Who is that who is loud?" Her husband responded, "Some nigger." I thought I heard the comment, but maybe I really didn't. I didn't say anything to my wife about the comment; I began processing what I thought I heard and what my course of action should be. A few seconds later, my wife said, "Did you hear him say "nigger?" I did not respond to my wife, but I immediately got up and *addressed* the white man's derogatory comment. The white man denied saying that and pointed in another direction as to where the comment originated. The bigot and his wife eased away from their seats to a more comfortable distance away from us.

Disrespect in the Barbados Airport

My wife and I were going through Customs in Barbados in 2018, and we were about to board our plane for our return flight to Cleveland. There were two separate Customs lines with boarders queued. Each line had its own Customs agent. When it came our turn, my wife was trying to find our paperwork in her purse. As my wife was searching her purse, an American white woman left her long line and attempted to jump in front of us.

The Barbadian Customs agent stopped the white woman in her tracks. She yelled, "Get back to your line! You will not disrespect them! Not in this country. You may do that in your country—but not here! The white woman retreated back to her line with nary a word of protest.

When the white woman was attempting to jump in front of us, we did not think much of it; we were accustomed to this type of arrogant behavior and I am sure that the white woman was too. It was thrilling to have this disrespect recognized and chastised.

Disrespect at Cleveland-Hopkins Airport

As my wife and I were standing in the packed aisle to de-plane from a flight from Washington, D. C. to Cleveland, a young white guy begin reaching for his luggage from an overhead bin that was at my face level. He was standing about two rows ahead of us, but he was stretching back trying to reach his bag. He reached right across my face in an attempt to retrieve his bag. He did not say, "Excuse me" or any other words. Since he didn't say anything, I did. I said to him in a very agitated tone, "Can't you say "Excuse me?" He said he did, but that was a lie. So his mother apologized for him and told him to just wait. Total disrespect. I was taught better manners than that.

I have observed that when a line has queued at the cash register in a store, white folks will not stand *directly* behind black people. White folks will stand behind but off to the side, almost to the point of cutting in front of the black person immediately in front of them. I have also noticed that when white folks and blacks are approaching an entry door from opposite directions and are equal distance from the door, white folks will almost break into an all-out sprint in order to be first. I surmise that white folks want to hold on to that contrived sense of superiority. This behavior may be a vestige of the "back of the bus" scheme that was so cleverly contrived in the segregated South in the '50s.

Disrespect in Meadville, Pennsylvania

I could go on and on, but I don't want to bore anyone. My son and I had driven up to Allegheny College in Meadville, Pennsylvania, several months ago for his official football visit. We drove up a day early so that we could spend the night at a hotel and be rested for the activities of the following day. The day of the official visit, we arose early and got dressed and left our hotel room to go eat breakfast.

As we were walking down the hallway to leave for breakfast, my son was walking a short distance behind me. A white man was approaching and I greeted him a warm, "Good morning." He did not respond at all as he kept walking down the hallway. This was in *2019* in *Pennsylvania*. I yelled out angrily, "You don't have to speak!" My response to him was very much tempered by the presence of my son.

Usually, when a white person and I are approaching, I put the onus on the white person to speak first—that way—I am not "feeling some type of a way" if the white person does not speak. My *nature* is to speak to whomever I meet; however, I have been conditioned by my experiences to oftentimes act contrary to my nature.

As a counterweight—to add balance—I will share with you two pleasant recent occurrences that happened in March 2020. My wife and I and a couple of good friends stopped at Cracker Barrel in Youngstown, Ohio, to have dinner. My friend Dewayne, who lived in Arizona for a while, speaks to *everyone*. While waiting to be seated, he struck up a conversation with this white woman stranger from Arizona. She was so nice and down to earth and invited us to visit her and her husband whenever we were in Arizona. She informed us quietly, that she was not like most other whites. She was extremely friendly.

A few days after the above incident, I was unloading groceries from my cart into the trunk of my car in Beachwood, Ohio. A young white woman was also unloading her grocery cart across from me. We finished about the same time and as we both began rolling our carts back to the store, she offered to take my cart back to the store also. I accepted the generous offer and thanked her for her kind and unexpected show of humanity.

I remember these latter two incidents because they were not common occurrences. Not only do I remember them, but I will *long* remember them. The sad part of all the occurrences that I have discussed above is that I will long remember the negative occurrences, too. Unfortunately, there are far too many of the negative occurrences to actually be balanced by the positive occurrences.

Living in a Predominantly White Suburb

I live in a mostly white suburb, but I do not know any of my white neighbors and I do not have an interest in knowing them. I know that as a church elder, I should not be saying that, but I have been *conditioned* over the years by my lifetime of experiences with being rejected, mistreated, disrespected, and hated by white folks because of the color of my skin. I have adopted an attitude of if you greet me first, then I will greet you in *return*. When I extend a greeting first and it is not returned, it leaves me "feeling some type of a way." Let me add though, that there are a handful of whites in the subdivision who do speak in passing in the neighborhood.

Maybe more whites would speak in passing if the energy that I give off was more inviting—maybe that's it! As I have said before, black people have the uncanny ability to size up a situation pretty quickly as we determine whether friend or foe. We may get it wrong sometimes, but it is better for us to err on the side of caution—if not for safety—for psyche.

My youngest son attends and is a senior at Orange High School in Pepper Pike, Ohio, a rather affluent high school in the area; he told me that his class overwhelmingly voted for Trump during a mock election. I was somewhat taken aback when my son told me of the mock election results, but really, I shouldn't have been—given my social experiences with expectations and disappointments. The people in this community appear to be quite well-off; they live in upscale homes, drive high-end vehicles, and seem to be professionals for the most part; they don't drive pick-up trucks or tractors, or carry lunch pails to work—they shower before work rather than after work. But, they vote for a person like Trump. You can put lipstick on a pig, but it is still a pig.

I have been a very keen observer of race and its many manifestations. I observe that, routinely, when there is a row of chairs in a waiting area and a black man is seated next to the only two empty chairs, the white man will sit next to the black man, with his white woman seated on the other side of him— that is if they sit down at all.

One more little observation, I have noticed that when some white folks approach black people, the white folks cough. What is that all about? Maybe it's just me being on high alert to instances of peculiar behavior related to race.

CHAPTER 6
Dorm and Campus Life

My first dorm assignment was to Saffold Hall. It was an older building, designed with a series of stairwells. At the top of each stairwell was a landing, with two dorm rooms on either side of the landing and a community shower in the middle and at the back of the stairwell. After my first white roommate fled within minutes of my entrance into the dorm room, I eventually was assigned a black roommate.

As I recall, only three of the four dorm rooms were occupied in the stairwell where my room was. Sam and Ted, I remember their names, were roommates—they were white; Arthur and Jerome were roommates, and Robert and I were roommates—all black. We never had any problems with Sam and Ted and we co-existed without incident in that dorm setup. We outnumbered them, but even if we had not, we were not the type of Negroes who would tolerate foolishness.

Recently, I interviewed Arthur Dunning, and we talked about Saffold Hall and the setup. He wondered aloud how the only four blacks in the entire dorm wound up living together in the same stairwell. We laughed because we thought it was funny how that worked out—what are the odds?

I remember one rainy afternoon, my roommate Robert and I were walking from our dorm over to Paty Hall to eat dinner. As we began passing some windows to Paty Hall, a white student poured water on us from a fourth floor window. We immediately dashed through the doors and up the stairs to the fourth floor to meet the perpetrator and extract an apology. Like I said, we were not the type of Negroes who would tolerate foolishness. To our disappointment, we failed to locate the perpetrator, but we never had that experience again.

Intramural Football

For some reason, it was not unusual for blacks to be seen playing intramural football alongside their white dorm mates during those times. Many of the dorms organized their own football teams and did not exclude blacks. News flash! "University of Alabama Integrates Its Dorm System Football Teams Years Before the Crimson Tide Did."

When we played against other dorms, there was never any kind of race-related problems of which I was aware. There was a certain acceptance in this setting, whereas in other settings, the acceptance was not quite so easy. I guess segregation is just funny that way.

I remember that I, as a wide receiver, drew up a pass play for me for the go ahead touchdown on the last play of an intramural game. The quarterback overthrew me and I remember his comment that I would "remember that play a long time"; he was right, but I remember it because of that comment. He overthrew me; I guess he thought that I should have been Super Negro and taken wings and caught up to his errant pass.

The Confederate Flag

After spending two years at Saffold Hall, I was assigned to Paty Hall—a newer male dorm—my junior and senior years. A few of our white dorm mates were friendly toward us and would associate with us as occasions permitted—they were mostly Northerners. I remember one such Northerner from Michigan who laughed and joked with us black dorm mates. This one particular day, we were in the hallway fooling around and his dorm room door came open and we could see that he had this huge Confederate flag on his wall directly opposite the door. The flag was as large as the wall on which it was displayed.

My black friends and I were so disappointed and taken aback by our white "friend." We understood exactly what the Confederate flag signified. We inquired as to why the flag and he tried to down play the significance of it. I don't know if he was trying to curry favor with the Southern whites by this ostentatious display of symbolic hatred for blacks or if he was attempting to identify with white Southerners' prevailing social mores and trying to fit in—when in Rome, do as the Romans do, or if he was a "redneck" at heart. Needless to say, the relationship between him and us cooled immediately.

This situation is reminiscent of the immigration of southern, eastern and central European "whites" that were looked upon as less than white and had to prove themselves and their whiteness by being even harder on black people. Be mindful that many Southerners really despised Northerners, but not as much as Southerners hated/despised blacks. Remember the Pace Picante Sauce commercial? The Southern diners decried the sauce because, "This stuff was made in New York City!" Maybe my Michigan white "friend" was trying to show, via the display of the gigantic Confederate flag, that he was a Southerner at heart and that his values were like unto theirs.

Friendly Whites

A handful of our Northern white dorm mates seemed not to care what other whites might think or say of their free association with us. I remember one white guy in particular, Thomas Sminkey from Hicksville, New York; he was a very cool white dude and also a walk-on on the football team. We engaged in conversations very comfortably. I even let him wear my double-breasted pinstripe suit to a homecoming game—we were the same size and the same build.

I have tried on several occasions to contact him, but to no avail. I even tried to reach him through my University of Alabama contact, but I did not get any hits. I would very much like to talk to him as old friends and to see where life has taken him.

Stillman College for Respite

After a week of attending classes and doing homework, many blacks would go home on the weekends if they lived reasonably close to campus. The campus was like a ghost town on weekends compared to the rest of the week, especially for the black students. Joining a fraternity was not even a thought.

Some weekends, if we could get a ride, we would travel up to Stillman College and hang out. Stillman College was a small historically black college (HBCU) established in 1867, about two miles from the University of Alabama. It was a place where we could really relax and have fun in a more receptive environment. Stillman had a female to male ratio of five to one, which made the two mile trip a big weekend attraction for us guys. I am not sure how our female Bama counterparts handled their weekends.

We got the feeling that some of the Stillman students resented us from coming on *their* campus for the purpose of socializing. Nothing was ever said explicitly, but implicitly we knew that some of the male students were not "feeling" us. We may have been perceived as trying to assimilate with whites and that we only came to socialize at Stillman because we had failed to successfully assimilate into white society. We could not, in good conscience, argue with their perception. We were in an in-between place.

Stillman College, in the 60s, had an awesome basketball team. Many of us blacks would oftentimes travel up to Stillman to watch their basketball team play. They played a more exciting brand of basketball—and so did the teams they faced—than did the Bama basketball team. We would forsake the Alabama basketball games, where we could get in for free just by presenting our student I.D. cards, to go pay and watch Stillman play. Stillman had a "run and gun" fast-paced offense, which was very exciting to watch for us blacks who were accustomed to this type of basketball. We were subconsciously connecting to our roots when we visited Stillman.

Pride and Resentment

I was proud to be a Bama student. I remember when I first enrolled at the University, I tried to buy all of the clothing that I could that contained the University of Alabama insignia; I guess that I wanted to publicize my *arrival*. I had never done my own laundry before. I remember the *crimson* colored sweatshirts. After the first wash, all of my white clothes were pink, but I was proud to wear the University of Alabama insignia. To me, it represented a certain level of distinction and achievement in the black community—even though some in the community might have looked on it as "trying to be white."

It is not unusual to be resented by some in the black community when one of their own succeeds or advances in the white world. Such attitudes are hurtful, but not hurtful enough to deter me. In my specific case, I wanted to go where I knew I wasn't welcome. I wanted to go because it was my *right* to attend the school of my choice in my home state. I refused and refuse to be denied what is rightfully mine.

The Making of a Man

The above anecdotal stories have helped mold me into the man that I am today. I have very few white friends or associates, and upon reflection, I can say that I actually do not have *any* white friends. However, I do have a couple of white associates, but they are in connection with business dealings.

I love *all* people. I sincerely wish and pray for the best for all people. In my prayers, I pray consistently and without ceasing that God will make this world a better place in which to live for every human being that has breath. I pray for a world in which the lion and the lamb can lie down together. With this as part of my worldview, I believe that I feel the sting of expressions of white superiority, discrimination, injustice, and meanness more deeply than many.

I am aware that the tone of this book is indicative of the constant conflict of my worldview and my love for my fellow man and the "is ness" in which we live. I am not writing to appease and paint rosy pictures; I am writing from the heart. I am writing in an attempt to prod America into living up to the words of its creed and its high ideals. When we read our Pledge of Allegiance and our Preamble to the Constitution, let the words be meaningful, let them be true.

Walking across campus to various classes, white students did not speak to us blacks as they did to other whites—Southern hospitality and cordiality were reserved for whites. Even the "wanna be" hippies did not speak. They pretended to be liberal with a free spirit, but their liberalism and spirituality did not extend to us. They might have been hippies, but they were Alabamians first.

I was involved in only one fight while at the University of Alabama. One Saturday night I was milling around downstairs in the dorm lobby at Paty Hall and this white guy looked a little inebriated and I said something to him jokingly; he came over to me and swung at me and I beat and wrestled him to the floor and he just laid out on the floor for a while. The following Monday, he sought me out and apologized to me. I later found out that he was from New York and he was at the university on a wrestling scholarship. The dorm counselor watched the whole thing unfold, but he did not intervene—go figure.

Doesn't it seem ironic that the one fight that I had while at the University of Alabama would be with a New Yorker? I don't think that his initiation of the fight was racially motivated—not totally. I think the main reason for the fight was his inebriated condition.

I am aware of only one other fight between a black student and a white student. This "fight" happened one evening in Paty Hall in the elevator. Loud yells for help could be heard coming from the elevator. When we arrived, we could see that one of our friends, Jessie, had been *beaten*; Jessie had been beaten by a white student who outweighed Jessie by at least 150 lbs.

We, my black friends, who had come to the scene of the beating were very angry and we discussed our different options. The beating was not reported to school officials and I don't know why. It may have been an unconscious thought that Jessie would not have received justice in that racial climate—I am not sure. The intensity of our anger subsided after a while, but this incident added to the plethora of negative experiences that we have with our white brothers. Occurrences like these make the man.

Remembering the Night That Dr. Martin Luther King, Jr. Was Assassinated

On the night that Dr. Martin Luther King, Jr. was assassinated, April 4, 1968, I was sitting in my Saffold Hall dorm room alone, shining a pair of black shoes. When I first heard the news, I couldn't believe what I had just heard; I continued shining my shoes as though I had heard no such news. A short time later, I began to process what I had just heard.

After absorbing the dreadful news, I went across the stairwell landing to Jerome's and Arthur's room and shared the devastating news; we were all stunned—not commenting very much. I believe that we were in a stupor—not wanting to believe what had just happened and contemplating the enormity of what this actually meant for our people and the country going forward. The assassination and funeral occurred around the time of mid-term exams. These events distracted us greatly from our preparation for our pending mid-terms—we studied while watching continuous news coverage of the funeral—trying to stay abreast of what was going on moment by moment.

It was a dreadfully sad time for our nation, at least for much of our nation. Fires and violence erupted across the United States. Blacks took to the streets to display their pent up anger. Black-friendly leaders who blacks had put their hope in for a better day—John Kennedy, Robert Kennedy, Martin Luther King, Jr.—all were assassinated *before* they could finish their work, work that would change American society for the better.

Experientially, I know that *change* and *changers* are oftentimes met with opposition and sometimes, deadly opposition. It appears that we hold on to the familiar and the comfortable even when the familiar and the comfortable are not worth holding on to. It seems that once we get a thing *our* way, we tenaciously deny the validity of any other way. Is it natural, innate for us to fight even righteous change once we have become comfortable with the way things are and the way things are benefitting us to the detriment of others? Is there a dangerous chemical reaction in the brain when change is afoot?

CHAPTER 7

Welcome to Alabama Football –
Peeping Through the Privacy Covers

During the spring of 1967, some of my friends and I were over near Thomas field—the Tide practice field—playing an intramural football game. When the game was over, my friends and I began looking through the gaps in the privacy covers that were attached to the chain link fence, erected to provide privacy while the Crimson Tide football team practiced. After watching the Tide practice for a while, I said excitedly, "I can do that!"   Sometimes when we *hear* about major or challenging things, we ascribe almost insurmountable obstacles or gigantean effort and enormous talent required to accomplish those things, but when we *see* the major or challenging thing being done by people like ourselves, we may come away with a doable spirit. The thing being done is within our reach. Some of us take it a step further; we actually do the thing.

When it was time for spring football practice, three of my other friends and I decided that we would try out for the team—we had heard that a black player from Montgomery, Dock Rone, had written to the famous coach and football icon, Paul Bear Bryant, asking permission to try out for the previously segregated team and he was granted permission. I wonder how many white players asked for permission to walk on.

Identification of The First Five

Before sharing my story with my wife in 2009, I had not shared my story with anyone in the 42 years since I left the team. I had not even talked to the other four black walk-ons: Dock Rone, Jerome Tucker, Arthur Dunning, and Melvin Leverett since graduating from the University of Alabama (Bama) in August, 1970. Dock Rone, a star, All-State high school football player, tried out for guard; Arthur Dunning, who had served in the United States Air Force, tried out at halfback; Melvin Leverett, who had the size of a college football player— 6'2", 230 lbs.—who is now deceased—tried out at fullback; Jerome Tucker and I walked-on as halfbacks, but were both later moved to wide receiver positions. Arthur, Jerome, and I were not physical specimens by any stretch of the imagination, but we possessed skills, heart, and courage. Dock and Melvin looked physically more like the idealized college football players of that era.

I wanted to play football since forever. Even before I entered the ninth grade, my best friend Rollie and I went out for the high school football team. We practiced for a while with the team until Coach Alfred Hall found out that we were only going to be in the eighth grade when the season started. I came back out for the team in the spring of my eighth grade year and I made the team and began playing in the fall in my ninth grade year; I played sparingly; however, I did throw a 29 yard touchdown pass in the first game in which I played—against a team which my brother coached.

I started at quarterback in my senior year and led my team to the Jefferson County championship game. I spent my junior year in Akron, Ohio, and did not play football that year. In the championship game, we loss 24-9 to the team coached by my brother; we had beaten them quite handily, 32-0, during the regular season.

I had good hands and decent speed. I was not going to be a quarterback at Alabama for obvious reasons—my color and my limited passing abilities. A black Bama quarterback in 1967 was not going to happen and my passing abilities were such that I could not compete successfully at that position at the college level. (Ken Stabler was *the* star quarterback when I walked-on.)

I was selected as a second team All-Conference halfback at the end of my senior year football season in high school. I never played running back. I think that the Jefferson County officials who decided those things thought that I deserved a spot somewhere since, as a quarterback, I had led my 7–1 team to the county championship game. I thought that my best chance for success was at halfback at Bama.

Walking into History

In an online article, dated June 6, 2012, titled "The 1967 Walk-ons: The Forgotten Pioneers of Alabama Football's Integration," writer C. J. Schexneyder states: "Until now, the presence of these five African-American athletes on the Alabama practice field has been seen as an outlier in the story of the integration of the football team. The narrative instead focuses on the offering the scholarship to basketball player Wendell Hudson in 1969, football player Wilbur Jackson in 1970 and the 1971 Alabama vs. USC game that saw John Mitchell take the field and, at long last, cross the Crimson Tide's varsity football color line.

"Yet, while the importance of these events cannot be overstated, neither can the contributions of the black walk-ons that preceded them. In a paper I delivered at the North American Society of Sports Historians' annual congress last week, I argue that there were a confluence of powerful factors in the spring of 1967 that finally forced the University of Alabama to take action.

"Thus, the presence of the five walk-on players at spring training was more than just another milestone on the way toward integration—it was the crossing of the Rubicon."

The five of us at some point decided to walk over to the football locker room together to present ourselves as football walk-ons; the locker room was adjacent to the practice field. As we walked in, all eyes were on us. The noisy locker room became as quiet as a well-run library. No one moved; no one uttered a word; we were the center of attention. We had not even talked among ourselves as to what to expect regarding our reception—we were so unassuming and naive.

While writing this, I wonder for the first time what the white players thought. In their wildest imagination, did they ever envision a day when the Tide locker room would not be lily white? Did the white players see us as a threat to the settled, contrived, dual construct of segregation and white superiority? Did the white players consider the cognitive dissonance that would be created in their minds if black athletes proved their equal or better? I'm just wondering.

The trainer, Coach Goostree, came out to meet us. Coach Goostree was surprisingly cordial with us and did not attempt to discourage us in any way. He handled our being there as just the normal course of performing his job. We told him why we were there and he took us over to the nearby University infirmary to get our physicals.

A few years ago, I tried to find Coach Goostree and I learned that he had passed away a few years prior. He was one of the people who I wanted to thank for just being civil with us. Coach Goostree did not appear uncomfortable with our presence—maybe he was quietly awaiting that particular experience.

We long remember acts of kindness embedded during those early years at Alabama. We also remember the people. We remember these acts and these people because they were so few and far between acts and people who were not so kind. We needed this as encouragement to keep going.

We all passed our physicals and when we returned to the locker room, we were all issued our football equipment. I have recently read some news accounts of those historic days when The First Five showed up for practice. The news accounts stated that only Dock Rone was allowed to participate in the first practice because the rest of us had to have our grades checked—

insinuating that there was a possibility that we might be academically ineligible. We were already admitted and enrolled and attending classes. How long would it take to check grades?

As Arthur, Jerome, and I recall it, there was no waiting at all, our grades were fine, and the five of us began practice on the same day. I recently read an old newspaper story in which Assistant Head Coach Sam Bailey said that the four of us had to wait to be checked out. Our accounts of the matter differ.

Invitees vs. Intruders

Those players who came years later were *invitees*—we five were *intruders*; thus, our story—our experience—might be just a bit different from what some might have heard from those who followed later or from those who wrote about the events years later using secondary and even tertiary sources. My story is my story; it is the testimony that has been built up in me over the years as a black man growing up in the South and treated as a second-class citizen. This may be a hard read for my white sisters and brothers, but it is a necessary read if we have any chance of moving forward via knowledge, acknowledgment, and a commitment to "act justly and to love mercy" (Micah 6:8); that is what the Lord requires.

It has been 53 years, as of this writing, since the events of 1967; quite a bit has been written, said, filmed, and speculated on regarding the events and attitudes during the *season* of desegregation at the University of Alabama. I present as not only an eyewitness, but a *participant* in the events and a *recipient* of vitriolic expressions and contempt.

Mild-Mannered Negroes

In an article in the *St. Petersburg Times*, the writer reported that the chairman of the Alabama athletic committee, Dr. J. Jefferson Bennett, told him/her that "...the Negroes informed the school ahead of time that they would go out for spring training. They did it as a courtesy and the school in turn encouraged them"—not so!

The characterization given by Dr. Bennett, if reported accurately, gives the false impression that we were a group of mild-mannered Negroes asking permission to proceed. At least four of us were not seeking permission—we were exercising our rights as citizens of Alabama—who had been disenfranchised for far too long. No University of Alabama official *ever* "encouraged" us to attend the University of Alabama, let alone go out for the football team. The only one of us First Five who asked for clearance in advance to try out for the team was Dock Rone; the rest of us just showed up at Thomas Field for our football equipment, contrary to Dr. Bennett's assertion. Believe me—things were not that rosy for black students at the University of Alabama in 1967 as Dr. Bennett described.

Making Ourselves Presentable

I remember that we were instructed to get rid of all facial hair—beards and mustaches. With most black men, mustaches and beards are cultural features and prideful features. Four of us black players discussed the finer points of this requirement among ourselves, but we reluctantly complied; Dock lived away from the rest of us four and he was not a part of some conversations in which the four of us routinely engaged. We all had facial hair—baby hair if you will— hair that had not yet turned black. Remember, most of us were just teenagers.

I remember when the white establishment wanted to ban Afro style hair for football players because the *style* supposedly presented a safety issue in that the functionality and effectiveness of the helmet would be compromised. I see a white-washing to make us more presentable, palatable, and acceptable to white folks—we certainly didn't want to make them uncomfortable.

By way of observation, I see that *very few* black television news and sports reporters wear mustaches or beards—I wonder why. I submit that facial hair and the length of one's hair or hair style have nothing to do with performance, but everything to do with prejudices, conformities, and comfort. It seems so paradoxical that they would be so concerned about our safety, while trying to keep us from even playing the game.

In this current era, black players in particular, wear a myriad of hairstyles, including Afros, dreads, etc. I am not aware of even one incident where a football player's hair style caused a head injury. A lie travels fast, but the truth catches up.

In the year 2020 A.D., a white high school official in the great state of Texas required that a black student cut off his dreads (hair style) as a condition for him to march across the stage to receive his high school diploma. A Mont Belvieu Texas high school official defended the schools demand by declaring that it was not the hair style per se, but the length of the hair. The student, in compliance with that length rule, always wore his dreads up and off his shoulders; but there came a time when that was not enough and the school required the student to cut his dreads as a precondition to marching across the stage for his high school diploma. Was the school and school official trying to make America great again? What was that all about?

By contrast to the Texas school hair rule, an *Associated Press* article of January 23, 2020, reported that:

"Last year, California became the first state to ban workplace and school discrimination against black people for wearing hairstyles such as braids, twists and locks. The state's governor signed the legislation into law in July." On the one hand you have Texas—a red state, and on the other hand you have California—a blue state.

Given Texas' and similarly situated red states' position on this hair issue, I proffer that these states will come around to the California way of thinking in about 40 years—maybe 30—if Trump is a one-term president. If history repeats itself, I envision apologies and platitudes from the offenders.

Remember the 1977 television miniseries *Roots* and the slave character Kunta Kinte played by LaVar Burton? The white slave master repeatedly inflicted physical harm on his rebellious slave because the slave would not accept the American name of "Toby." The tri-fold purpose of changing Kunta's name to the American name was to strip Kunta Kinte of *his* rightful name, to strip him of his non-slave identity, and to show him and other blacks that the white man is in charge and is calling *all* of the shots.

White folks must understand that they are not the gold standard in this vast multi-cultural/multi-national world. Whiteness does not equate with quintessence. Live and let live. Do not deny people their liberty and pursuit of happiness just because you can. There *will* come a day when white folks will not be in the superior position that they are in now and they would no doubt prefer that those in power be more tolerant and kind to them.

Football Practices

Practices were rigorous, as could be expected. Each day at the beginning of practices, players would read from a posted roster the particular team that they were assigned to for that day; there were several gradations of skill level associated with each team. Each day, team assignments were posted on a bulletin-type board; the team to which a player would be assigned could vary from day-to-day.

The color of the jersey corresponded to the team to which players were assigned. The jersey colors were red, white, yellow, green, orange, and so forth. Red jerseys signaled first team, white jerseys signaled second team, and so forth. Colors also denoted whether offense or defense.

As I remember it, team assignments were not very fluid, but could vary. If a player performed exceptionally well on a particular day or for a particular period, he could move up a jersey color. On the other hand, if a player performed particularly poorly, he could move down a jersey color.

There were about eight conjoined practice fields, two abreast, with Coach Bryant's tower in the middle. As I recall it, there were about twice as many coaches as there were practice fields. The number of coaches was impressive to me; it was the first time I had experienced specialized position coaches. When I was in high school, we had one coach; he coached football, basketball, baseball, and track. Such were the times at my all-black high school.

Coach Bryant, bull horn in hand, mainly coached from his tower. The tower allowed him to clearly view all of the practice fields and players and coaches. I rarely heard him correct a player directly; if the assistant coaches did not address the errant player immediately, Coach Bryant would jump on the assistant coach, over his bull horn, for the assistant coach's failure to provide a corrective response to the errant player.

When we had team meetings in an auditorium-like room, Coach Bryant commanded the meetings. Sometimes, his Southern drawl and low monotone would be difficult for even other Southerners to understand. Assistant coaches *never* asked Coach Bryant to repeat what he had said because they did not hear him clearly; the assistant coaches would invariably quietly ask each other, "What did he say?" Now, that's reverence!

Along the way, Arthur and Melvin decided to concentrate on their education and were not on the team at the time of the 1967 intra-squad A-Day game. Only three of us remained through the 1967 annual A-Day intra-squad game. Contrary to many news accounts, I did not suit-up for my first A-Day game, but Jerome Tucker and Dock Rone did. I was disappointed but not defeated.

Although I thought I had performed well enough to be selected to suit-up for the A-Day game, I was told to come back next football season—and I did. I thought that at the time that for appearance sake—not all of the black players (3) should be selected to play in the A-Day game because not all the white players were selected to play. It's just fair—isn't it?

I came back for the following season and I was the only returning black player. I am not quite sure why Dock and Jerome did not return. I continued to practice hard and I did play in the following spring A-Day game in 1968. I played three downs at flanker, but no action was directed my way. I returned for the following 1968 fall practice.

The Scout Team and How Tucker and I Became Flankers

One day while practicing, Coach Bryant asked the assistant coach who was working with the halfbacks to arrange for Ken Stabler and another quarterback to each throw Jerome (Tucker) and me some passes. We both caught the two long passes that were thrown to each of us. As I recall it, my passes were both fingertip catches. The experience was surreal; I ran as fast as I could and caught up with the two long passes that had been thrown to me.

I had no choice but to catch the passes as I perceived that this would be a pivotal moment in regards to our football futures and maybe to the futures of others. After that, Coach Bryant had Jerome and I run two 40-yard wind sprints against each other; Jerome won the first sprint and I won the second sprint. As a result, we became flankers, aka wide receivers—after that point. For those who do not remember the term "flanker," the flanker is a pass receiver who normally lined-up in the slot or out wide.

The five of us were relegated to the Scout Team; the Scout Team scrimmaged the regular players each day. Alabama had "scouts," which I am sure all teams did and do; Alabama scouts routinely scouted opposing teams to learn their plays, personnel, and formations. Our job as Scout Team members was to run the scouted plays against our starters to prepare them for the next game with the respective opponents.

One day while scrimmaging, I ended up on defense—at linebacker—150 lbs. I am not sure why the coach put me in on defense, much less at linebacker. I surmise that it was just a confluence of events that caused this situation. The big 225 lb. pound husky fullback came busting up the middle; I reacted by meeting him head-on with a block below the knees. I knocked him into a head over heels flip. *Everyone* was amazed at this event. I guess that the coaches had expected to have a good laugh after the fullback ran me over, but there was no laughter to be heard—just silent awe.

When I was an underclassman in high school, I was known for *hitting*. I teach my youngest son now, don't just tackle—*hit*! I instinctively reacted to the fullback full steam up the middle. As I teach my son, size doesn't matter when you put on the football uniform, you are a *football player* period.

Where Did All the News Reporters Go in the Fall of 1967?

In the beginning, news coverage at the Bama practice field was heavy—reporters were all over the place covering us five black players, until one day they *all* stopped coming at once—as if they had been instructed to not come back.

The First Five were oblivious as to what was being said in the media about our brazenness. We did not follow media accounts involving our audacity—at least I didn't. We had zero consideration for the long-lasting impact that we were making nor for the worth of our actions. We mainly wanted to play football as we pursued our education at *our* university. I only learned several years ago from various media, the extent to which we caused a disturbance.

As I think about it many years later, I ponder the reason for the sudden cessation of news coverage at the practice field. One might reasonably expect that all news reporters would not leave on the same day—that their numbers would dwindle down to zero over a few weeks.

I have subsequently and very recently learned from a closer reading of Coach Bryant's 1970 deposition, that he had a hand in the cessation of the presence of reporters. He mentioned that the presence of the reporters created a *safety* problem for us black players. Could it be that the presence and the reporting of the reporters created and sustained a public awareness of the *presence* of The First Five or did the sustained coverage become a sustained aggravation for the citizenry?

CHAPTER 8
Players and Coach Who Stood Out

The Ken Stabler Affect

There was only one player who greeted me on a frequent basis— Ken Stabler. He was the star quarterback and *big man* on campus and went on to star with the Oakland Raiders, the Houston Oilers, and the New Orleans Saints. He always made it a point to speak to me as I entered the locker room. He would always say, "How 'bout it Pernelli?" As I think of it today, I believe that *his* speaking to me, influenced other players to *tolerate* my presence and to not be outwardly antagonistic toward me—Ken Stabler was top dog.

From my sociology classes, I learned that a person of high position or standing can more freely interact—casually—with a person of perceived lower degree or standing without having this interaction viewed as unacceptable by those in the dominant group. Similar interactions by a person in the dominant group with lesser position or standing would be frowned upon by members of the dominant group for similar interactions.

The name "Pernelli" stuck; everyone, including the coaches, called me "Pernelli." My name even appeared on the daily practice rosters as "Pernelli." I wondered if the addition of the "i" to my last name gained traction because it carried a subliminal message of possible Italian extraction. Maybe it helped some cope with the reality or maybe the use of "Pernelli" was used in a well-meaning endearing way. It may very well have been the latter, but within the context of the times, it caused me to suspect the former.

One day in 2012, Ken Stabler—out of the blue—called me on my cell phone as I was driving back from Alabama to Ohio. I had been trying to get in touch with him for quite a while to express my gratitude and sincere appreciation for the friendly way in which he responded to me during the early years, but my efforts had been unsuccessful. Somehow, he had gotten my number and we talked briefly as I was driving back.

No doubt someone had told Ken that I had expressed fond memories of him when I was speaking at a 2011 symposium at the University of Alabama. I thanked him for being civil and warm towards me when others would not even speak. I asked him, what made him so different from the others. He shared with me that he grew up around black people and he basically said "people are people." Those words are so simple, but yet so powerful and deep.

Observation! Live your life such that people will remember you fondly. I am sure that Ken called me because of the good—and *true*—things that I said about him. These acts of kindness, over 50 years ago—when his acts of kindness were out of season—have outlived him, at least in *my* mind. It is good to do *right* in season and out of season; if you do, history will be kind to you.

Ken Stabler grew up in Foley, Alabama, a very small, rural Southern town. I imagine that his home town was not atypical of other small, rural Southern towns in the 1960s. I thanked him personally when he was alive and I thank him now, posthumously, for his courage and his humanity. I suspect that there were other "Ken Stablers" on the team, but I will never know—they remained silent in their acquiescence to tradition and peer pressure.

In my interviews with four former football players who I thought qualified as decent people, I noticed a common thread among them. They all grew up around black people, albeit with black people in subservient positions. I wonder if the early familiarity with black people caused them to be more comfortable around and less prejudiced toward black people. Oftentimes, we fear the unknown and we have ample evidence of what fear can breed, birth, and nurture.

Even with the Southern traditions and customs, some people rise above traditions and customs and do what's right and just. What is it that allows right and justice to triumph over traditions and customs in some and not in others? I submit that *courage* plays a major role.

I have often commented that many white folks who live a rural, agrarian type lifestyle—far removed from black people—harbor racist ideas and attitudes that are far out of proportion to any actual threat. Their dealings with black people or even the likelihood that they would come in contact with black people are remote, yet they harbor negative feelings about black people. They don't even *know* us. I suspect that these are many of the same people who want the wall built—many of them are far removed from our Southern border. I posit that fear of the unknown is oftentimes greater than the thing feared.

Recently, in 2020, Woods Cross High School students in Utah, began chanting, "Build that wall!" while holding a Trump sign at a football game. This incident validates my point in the previous paragraph. These rural, lily white students, far, far removed from the brown people at the border—harbor racist ideas and attitudes. The chances of these white students coming face-to-face with any of these brown people is very remote.

Trump has stoked the dormant fires of hatred and fanned the flames of simmering racism to such a point that I don't think the nation will ever recover. What Trump has been able to achieve will take generations to undo, if indeed it can be undone. The only good part of what Trump has nurtured is that, now we know. We know who is friend and who is foe; we know that this is not a Christian Nation; we know that racism is not dead; we know that ours is not a post-racial society; we know that white privilege exists, we know that affirmative action is still needed—now we know.

Sam Gellersted—A Private Testimony

One other such player had demonstrated that courage, Sam Gellersted. One day Sam came up to me in the locker room in *private* and said in his Southern dialect, "Y'all are just as good as we are. If my daddy knew I said that, he'd kill me"; I believe that I said "Thanks" as he walked away. That's all that he said. We had not spoken to each other previously or since—until a few years ago. His statement caught me by complete surprise.

I already knew the truthfulness of Sam's declaration and that was the underlying reason that I chose to attend the University of Alabama. I appreciated the goodwill gesture and his courage for sharing that thought with me, even though it was in private—it was still a courageous show of humanity. I wonder, how many more "Sams" were on the team.

I found Sam's contact information on Facebook about four or five years ago and I contacted him—it had been about 40 years since that locker room talk or any other contact with him; however, he still remembered me and seemed genuinely glad to hear from me. We talked very briefly and I brought to his remembrance his words to me in the locker room at the University of Alabama in 1967; he lightly acknowledged the occurrence and had nothing more to say about that.

I was expecting more commentary from him regarding the matter. I believe that he was in the company of co-workers and maybe he did not wish to talk further about the locker room event while at his place of work. I was hoping that we could have had a serious talk about our times at the University, but it was not to be at that time. I sensed that Sam was at work and that he was reluctant to talk openly; he agreed to talk again later.

I had never divulged Sam's name, until now, for fear that his dad might still be of a mind to kill him if he found out what his son had said to me in the locker room in 1967. In February, 2015, I conducted a long and rewarding phone interview with Sam and he gave me permission to use his name. Sam too had contact and interactions with blacks growing up. Sam shared that his dad held racist beliefs, but that his dad was a kind man to *everyone*. Sam's assertion regarding his dad, validates my point that individual acts of kindness can be performed by racists. What I see here is that *learned* negative attitudes and behaviors oftentimes usurp or "Trump" our God-given essence.

I must share with you that out of all the years that I played football, Sam hit me harder than anyone else by far. We were scrimmaging two on two: Two defensive down linemen and two offensive down linemen and a running back—me. As I dashed toward the open hole, the hole began to close quickly as Sam slid off his block and hit me so hard that he knocked mucus from my nose. He was only 5'8" and 190 lbs. playing defensive line; I likened the severity of the hit to the sensation that a pedestrian might feel after being hit by a *small* truck head-on. Sam became an All-American at Bama in 1968 and at the University of Tampa in 1970 and 1971.

Dickey Thompson—Mean

There was only one player who was overtly hateful, and that was defensive back Dickey Thompson. We had a shoving match at practice one day that was started by him. He shoved me after the play was over and I responded in-kind. My response was automatic—I stood my ground; it may have set the tone for what others could expect if they behaved like Dickey. This act may have been the genesis for the future "stand your ground" laws.

I was not a big guy, but neither was Dr. Martin Luther King, Jr. or United States Congressman John Lewis, but they fought and were successful. I had fight in me and I still do. The old adage, "It is not the size of the dog in the fight, but the size of the fight in the dog," is still true today.

I identify Dickey by name so that he can get the credit for his actions and attitude. He didn't call me "nigger" or say anything at all, but I could read his eyes and the scowl on his face—akin to Coach Mal Moore's scowl.

As I said before, black people, for survival purposes, have to be able to read quickly the whites who they encounter. I hope that he has changed his attitude and ways and I hope that he will read this and will want to contact me and apologize for his actions. I reached out to Dickey, via email, some 48 years later, but I received no response. I may have read him wrongly, but I don't think so.

A Show of Acceptance-An Act of Kindness

Even though only one player was overtly hateful, *almost* all of the others were aloof. I said "almost." There was one lineman, whose name I do not remember, who wanted to measure his hand and finger length against mine and he commented that my hand and fingers were almost as long as his. Given my size compared to his size, this was a compliment and a goodwill gesture. I had excellent hands at my flanker position and I surmised that he was curious as to how a 5'8" player could snag passes like I was doing.

This seemingly insignificant event is remembered by me 53 years later. The event stood out and is long-remembered because of the humanity and the reaching out that he showed toward me in an environment otherwise almost void of any notice of my existence or my humanity. I wished I could remember his name so that I could recognize him in this book for his display of humanity out of season.

The distance that most of the white players placed between us via facial expressions and behaviors implied rejection. Some might say, well, that was good for the times, but it was not good for me. Remember, I was a 19-year-old *human being*; humans need social interactions and feelings of belonging. On the third rung of Maslow's Hierarchy of Needs, is "belonging," situated just below *physical* and *safety* needs.

Dennis Homan

Recently, I was reading some of the old newspaper articles from that 60s era and I came across a comment by former Tide wide receiver Dennis Homan that was reported in the *St. Petersburg Times* (April 13, 1967): "I'm not too much for integration but I don't see any use in fighting it. You don't have to buddy around with them (Negroes). If they're good enough to make the team, I'm for them. I think it would be great if one of the Negroes did make the team."

When I first read this article, I evaluated it as being totally negative. I was thrown off balance by the comment that "You don't have to buddy around with them." My defenses sprang up. On a later read of the article, I began to read it with a more critical eye.

Ambivalent, I suspect, is a good word to capture the essence of Dennis Homan's comments and feelings. In one sense, he seemed to be against integration in social settings. In another sense, he seemed to be more in favor of *desegregation* in sports settings and team play. Homan seemed to have a segregationist mentality in terms of race *mixing* and a *desegregationist* mentality in terms of sports participation. Note that there is an important nuanced difference between *integration* and *desegregation*—the characteristic of one is acceptance and the characteristic of the other is tolerance, respectively.

In retrospect and critical reading of Homan's comments, I must not allow his overall comment to overshadow his statement that, "If they're good enough to make the team, I'm for them." This statement is counterintuitive, but it is a courageous *public* statement given the times.

Desegregation may be the logical precursor to integration, a kind of not too much at one time, phase-in strategy. Being a "Christian Nation," integration of the races from the outset would seem to have been a no-brainer. It is extremely appalling that some white men contrived and constructed a perpetuating system of segregating the races in such a fashion that the system worked to the total benefit and aggrandizement of the white race and to the total subjugation and detriment of the black race. The resulting *false* sense of superiority may very well be the reason for not wanting to "buddy around" with us.

Coach Mal Moore

Coach Mal Moore was the only coach, of whom I am aware, who let his feelings be known as to how he felt about the presence of black players being on the mighty Crimson Tide football team. The other coaches were just coaches—showing no resentment. Growing up black in white America, especially in Alabama, blacks quickly learn—and it is imperative—to understand subtle signals, signs, attitudes, and expressions.

Although we, or at least I, never had any significant conversation with an assistant coach, I could feel that some of them silently cheered for us being there; however, silence adds to the length of the moral arc. The coaches were *coaches* and behaved as coaches often do—like drill sergeants—where *everybody* gets treated like soldiers going through basic training; however, Coach Mal Moore failed to contain his emotions sufficiently in relation to the presence of black players.

I remember one incident in particular. I sprained my ankle during practice one day; I had my ankle wrapped and I continued to practice. I subsequently stumbled during a running play. Coach Moore's stinging words, oozing out deep-seated hatred and the scowl on his contorted face, were verbalized in, "If you can't stand up, you need to get from out here!" Was that enough reason to suggest that I leave the team because I stumbled? I was afraid that he would bust a gut—but I was not really afraid—but hopeful. One more instance of white folks wishing that I go elsewhere.

Coach Moore had such a scowl on his face, as though he didn't want me "out here." His words were reminiscent of the University registrar's advice to me to go "somewhere else." There is more than one way to say "nigger" and all that it connotes, without verbalizing the word. As blacks, we intuitively understand the connotation of the facial expressions, tone, and body language of whites. This gift is used as a self-preservation mechanism, which allows us to *quickly* distinguish friend from foe.

Coach Moore may not have been a racist, but that's how I perceived him. I do not remember any other incidents like the one just mentioned, but really, how many incidents like this are needed for one to qualify as a racist? As I said earlier, blacks learn quickly who is friend and who is foe; it is essential to survival. My research revealed that Mal Moore was born in tiny Dozier, Alabama (2.97 square miles), with a population in 1990 (as far back as the census goes) of less than 500 and a current population of just over 300. Including this fact here will make sense later in this book and it will give the reader something to ponder.

I remember bumper stickers during the time George Wallace was running for governor of Alabama; the bumper stickers read, "Give 'em hell George." We knew—and they knew—who "em" referred to without having to have "em" explained; the context of the times *demanded* that we understand certain words, expressions, and body language. This slogan seemed to infer that we (blacks) were not *already* catching enough hell in Alabama. I felt like I was already going through enough hell without Coach Mal Moore turning up the heat. Fifty years later, we still get "Trumped."

I talked to Coach Bryant one-on-one on only one occasion. I met him as I was coming to practice one afternoon in 1968 as he was leaving the practice facility. I don't remember the conversation, but I was late and missed practice completely because no one told me that the team practiced early on Tuesdays; I subsequently found out that it had been arranged for all the scholarship players to practice early and have their labs later in the afternoon. I told him that I was unaware of the early practice times on Tuesdays. He kind of shrugged his shoulders in an understanding way and kept walking. I did not get the impression that he would offer me a ride if he saw *me* walking to practice.

This was the only football practice that I ever missed or showed up to tardy. This is what happens when there is no communication. It seemed that everyone knew about the early Tuesday practices but me. I was the only black on the team at this time in 1968.

CHAPTER 9

The Matter of the Academic Scholarship – Coach Sam Bailey

At some point during the fall practices of 1968, Assistant Head Coach Sam Bailey called me into his office. I was surprised that Coach Bailey would want to meet with me; I had no idea what the subject of the meeting could be. He informed me that the team had *discovered* that I was receiving an academic scholarship and that it was against SEC rules to participate in athletics while receiving an academic scholarship. I think that there were some news accounts that used the term "discovered" regarding my academic scholarship.

The inference was that I had hidden this academic scholarship fact from the University of Alabama. I was never asked whether I was on an academic scholarship; there was no form—of which I was aware—that players had to fill out that included this question. There may have been such a form, but I was unaware of such a form and I certainly did not complete such a form that hid the fact that I was on academic scholarship. No one ever *asked* me if I was on academic scholarship; that would have been the quickest and easiest way to *discover* whether I was on academic scholarship. This scholarship was not awarded at the beginning of my college career; it was awarded during either my sophomore or junior year and I may already have been on the team before the academic scholarship was awarded.

During the summer months of 1964 and 1965, I attended a Summer Study Skills Program (SSSP) at Knoxville College in Knoxville, Tennessee at the end of my sophomore and junior years in high school. The program was sponsored by the United Presbyterian Church of America. Dr. Ernst Suerkin was in charge of the overall program, but Mr. Samuel Johnson and his wife operated the program.

The program selected academically promising, *disadvantaged* youth from the South to participate. During both summers, we, the SSSP students, honed our skills in reading, math, English, and library usage. Two students were selected from my high school in Brighton to participate in the program both summers; Fred and I were the two selections.

The board of the United Presbyterian Church of America offered me a scholarship at some point during my matriculation at the University of Alabama and I gladly accepted the scholarship. The point of the program was to ameliorate some of the *disadvantages*—educationally—of growing up poor and black.

Not only did we improve our academic acuity, but we broadened our worldview by being exposed to cultural events. We took a trip to Cherokee, North Carolina to attend the Indian pageant, *Unto These Hills*. We traveled by chartered bus to New York City to see the Broadway play, *Golden Boy*, starring Sammy Davis, Jr. We were taken out to nice restaurants to eat each Saturday—reserved for those who had no grade lower than a "B" during the week, and we attended vespers every Sunday afternoon.

In his 1970 deposition, Coach Bryant referred to the scholarship as deriving from some "church," which minimized the value and significance of the scholarship. The scholarship was offered by *the* prestigious United Presbyterian Church of America. It was no small "church." In 1965, the United Presbyterian Church of America claimed a membership of 4,250,000.

Coach Bailey gave me a choice of sorts—give up my academic scholarship and stay on the team or keep my academic scholarship and leave the team. I had never considered leaving the team, even though having the chance to play in a game was very remote; however, I did come close to suiting-up for an actual game once. As I remember it, a player was hurt who played my same position. Coaches came around asking me what size shoes I wore and other uniform measurements. I was excited to the point where I called my parents and told them that I might be playing on Saturday. As quickly as the news reporters at practice left, so did hints of me playing in the Saturday game.

Coach Bailey had presented to me what amounted to a *Hobson's choice*. As I pondered briefly my chances of ever playing and my dependency on my academic scholarship, I decided to leave the team and keep my academic scholarship. Strangely, I felt some relief, and at the same time, some disappointment—relief from the grind of football with no real hope of playing in games and my disappointment that all my efforts had been in vain—it seemed to me at the time.

It was a bit ironic that I, a black academic scholarship player, would be forced to leave the team for having an *academic* scholarship. The player for which they had been searching the countryside for so long was in their midst—academically *and* athletically qualified. Even if I was not a "blue chip" athletically, it would seem that the combination of my dual qualifications would have motivated them to make extraordinary efforts to keep me—even if it was just to take the pressure off Coach Bryant and the University.

Free at Last!

When I exited Coach Bailey's office, I felt free. I felt as though a heavy burden had been lifted from my shoulders—a burden that I didn't know that I was carrying. Had I been unconsciously carrying the boarding passes for all of the black athletes who would follow later who wanted to ride the Crimson Tide?

I could not just quit—quitting was never a consideration; however, when the academic scholarship issue arose, it allowed me to *leave* without feeling as though I had a *real* choice in the matter. If I had stayed on the team, I could not have afforded the tuition without the aid of my academic scholarship. I had accomplished what I could and I had given my best effort. It was time for me to move on with my life.

I rarely talked about my experiences at the University of Alabama with anyone—that included my wife. I didn't think that my experiences were remembered by anyone and that I merely chalked them up to "experience" as opposed to "trailblazing." Thus, I didn't think that they were really worth mentioning and if I did mention them to anyone, I'd have had to give a long

account of what had happened in order for the listener to appreciate what
had happened.

The Value of a 1970 Degree from the University of Alabama

After graduating from the University of Alabama in 1970, my attempts to find
employment locally failed. Immediately after graduation, I interviewed for
employment at United States Steel in Fairfield, Alabama. I was told by my
employment interviewer that I qualified for a clerical job and that there would
be no room for advancement (for this University of Alabama graduate with a
fresh Bachelor's degree in Industrial Relations).

Goodbye Alabama, hello Ohio. Eight days later, I was on a Greyhound
bus to Akron, Ohio, to offer my job skills in that environment. It was a bit
ironic in that my degree from such a prestigious university did not carry much
weight at that time, even in Ohio. I believe that employment interviewers
outside the South didn't even consider that the "University of Alabama" on
my resume really was *the* University of Alabama—maybe thinking that blacks
did not even *attend* the University of Alabama; the interviewers' mindset
probably allowed them to mentally substitute the name of one of the
historically black colleges and universities, namely, Alabama State University
or Alabama A&M University for the university that I listed on my resume. I
hasten to add that these latter two universities are great universities and have
produced some great people; however, I had graduated from a university that
carried more prestige at that time—at least in the broader society.

It would have been a reasonable question to ask, "Which university?" But I
surmise that political correctness would not allow the job interviewers to go down
that road; I certainly didn't mention that I played football for the Crimson Tide—
that would probably have been laughable. During that time, for a black person
to graduate from *the* University of Alabama was akin to—prestige-wise—a white
person graduating from Harvard University—at least in the minds of many in
the black community. My point here is that my degree from the University of
Alabama did not enhance my opportunities in the job market at that time because
everyone knew that blacks didn't attend the University of Alabama—let alone
graduate from the University of Alabama during those times.

CHAPTER 10
Distortion, Reality, and Validation

The *St. Petersburg Times* (4/13/67) – Got It All Wrong

From a perusal, many years later, of an article in the *St. Petersburg Times* (April 13, 1967), entitled "Outdated Color Scheme: Lily-White Crimson Tide," I observed how a seemingly well-meant article can distort reality, give the unsuspecting and uncritical public a false sense of "all is well," and perpetuate stereotypes. On balance, the article does more harm than good. The article is likened unto *comfort* food. It makes you *feel* good, but it contributes to your *heaviness*.

The *St. Petersburg Times* (4/13/67) - "The First Five Were Not Athletic Standouts"

The *St. Petersburg Times* reporter makes light of the football credentials of The First Five, as though to provide an excuse for the University of Alabama in advance, if none of us made the team. Now that we had been *proven* academically qualified and nixed the stereotype that blacks could not qualify academically, our athletic prowess was called into question. While the reporter concerned himself/herself with our *chances* of making the team, we were fighting for a *chance* to make the team. In the writer's slightly veiled defense of a segregated Crimson Tide football team, he/she moves from academic qualifications to athletic prowess as lacking in combination in black students/athletes. Shameful!

Observe how the writer in the *St. Petersburgh Times* article supported the status quo—the segregation power structure—ever so subtly. The reporter began by declaring how graciously the white players treated The First Five; he/she continued by asserting that there were no protests around the state; he/she reluctantly and timidly stated that Coach Bryant could have been stronger in his integration attempts, but the reporter quickly empathized with Coach Bryant: "Well, I guess but it must have been hard to live in those shoes." What about *my* shoes!

Bonafide Crimson Tide Football Player or Not?

On a couple of occasions over the years, I've had a couple of high school classmates ask, "Didn't you play football at Alabama?" I would respond with a casual, "Yes", without going into any detail because it would have been a long story trying to adequately describe "What had happened was…" I guess I didn't think others would believe the story because there had been very little publicity about it since that era—to my knowledge at the time—so I just left it alone.

Since I didn't play in an official game that counted, I couldn't really *claim* that I played football for the University of Alabama—or could I? Some might argue that if I never played in an official contest, then I really didn't play football for Alabama—I won't argue the point. Whether or not I *played* football for the Crimson Tide, I was part of that mosaic of social change that exploded in the 60s.

Coach Bryant's Validation

In 1970, the Afro-American Association of the University of Alabama, Plaintiffs, filed suit against Paul "Bear" Bryant, et al, Defendants, to force integration of the Crimson Tide football team. Plaintiffs' attorney asked Coach Bryant to clarify the term "varsity." Bryant responded to the question from Plaintiffs' attorney: "Well, varsity, of course, people that help us win or lose; however, we think we consider everybody out for the team a candidate for the team, as part of the Varsity Team, because although they may not be playing, they are helping you in your preparation, running the other team's offense and defense and so forth…" "Now, those persons who play on Varsity Teams, but who do not actually play an intra-college game—well, they are members of the scout team; they don't play on the varsity team, they are members of the squad; if they don't actually play in the contest, intercollegiate contest" (pages 47 and 48 of the original complete deposition). Now, I guess it's fair to say that I was a bonafide Crimson Tide football player.

University of Alabama A-Club

Seemingly out of the blue on July 15th of 2014, Ralph Stokes, former Bama football standout and member of the A-Club committee, contacted me. Ralph informed me that A-Club board members, including Head Coach Nick Saban, had *unanimously* voted for my induction as an honorary member of the University of Alabama's prestigious A-Club, which is reserved for University of Alabama athletes who have lettered in any sport. A-Club head Jerry Duncan subsequently called with the details of the induction ceremony that was scheduled for April, 2015; however, the award itself was voted on in 2014.

As I reflect on the proposition that I was not a bonafide football player for Alabama, my gratification comes from knowing that I am now recognized as a "pioneer." How much courage do you think that it took to do what The First Five did? I cherish the label of *pioneer* and I like how *Dictionary.com* defines a "pioneer" as "a person who is among those who first enter or settle a region, thus opening it for occupation and development by others."

All Is Well?

It should be noted that *The St. Petersburgh Times* article appeared as a "Special to the Times," from *The Los Angeles Times*. An excerpt from the article: "Each day they scrimmage, share lockers and drink fountains with 150 white teammates and not a single voice around the state has been raised in protest"; does this statement seem plausible, given the state of Alabama's history? "The five Negroes out for football say they have not been harassed, taunted or treated with anything but courtesy in the locker rooms and on the playing field."

This article gives the impression that the five black players were not only accepted by their white teammates, but well-integrated into the team. In addition, the article claimed that there had been no protests against our being on the team. Isn't it funny how white folks—even well-meaning white folks—want so badly to make things appear much better than they are and to minimize the egregiousness of past sins? I don't know who this reporter talked to, but he certainly did not talk to me. His statement had no relationship or familiarity with reality or the truth.

The Reality

The reality of the team situation was *desegregation*. We were there; there was no camaraderie between black and white players—just distance. I can remember only a handful of players who even spoke to me during the spring and fall of 1967 and the spring and fall of 1968. There was no sharing of lockers—just the locker room.

As a matter of fact, I talked to the player who had a locker next to mine for the first time in 2015 when I was being inducted as an honorary member of the prestigious University of Alabama's A-Club. He came up—48 years later—and *introduced* himself and informed me that his locker was next to mine when we were playing football. He was very friendly and talkative; he even bragged to his young son that he shared a locker next to mine; I wish that he had been so cordial 48 years ago. He was probably the same friendly and talkative person back then, but perhaps the traditions and shackles of segregation had silenced him and kept him from expressing his humanity.

I conducted an interview with him, via phone, a few years ago. He was extremely helpful and forthcoming in the interview. He seems to be the kind of guy I would have wanted as a friend—segregation, traditions, and expectations were successful in keeping us apart even though the separation was not what I wanted and I suspect—that it was not what he wanted either. Wouldn't it be real funny if we find out that *most* whites did not really want the system of segregation and that they outnumbered those who did? See what happens when good people say nothing!

Hate Mail

The *St. Petersburg Times* article claimed that there had been no outcry or protests to our presence. To the contrary, as evidenced in part by four hate letters that I received during that time. I received four hate letters from "friends" of the University. The letters were addressed to: General Delivery, Andrew Pernell, Football Player, University of Alabama. I remember one letter in particular—they were all in the same vein—"Dear Nigger: Colored stars not wanted at Alabama. In other words, haul your black ass North." This letter had a typed signature, "V. C. Boticelli" and was postmarked "Tampa, Fla." Unfortunately or fortunately, over the years, all of these letters were lost. If anyone is offended by my *use* of the word "Nigger," then think how I must have felt being *called* "Nigger" and being *treated* like a "Nigger."

I wonder what old V. C. is doing today. Is he at a Trump rally? Was he at the white gun rally in Virginia on January 20, 2020? Does he cheer for the many starting black players who are now, and have been for quite a while, an integral part of the Crimson Tide football team? Maybe he's dead, along with his hatred for me and people "colored" like me. Colored stars not *wanted* at Alabama, but *needed*. Huh.

This letter was representative of the tenor of the times; the aforementioned comments in the *St. Petersburg Times* were just wishful thinking—another example of a white reporter telling the story that *he wanted* to tell or maybe it was an instance of poor investigative work.

I wonder what these racist letter writers are up to now. Did they cheer for Bama's black quarterback in the 2015 national championship game? How are they handling the truth?

The A-Club Recognition and Experience

I was invited to speak at the A-Club ceremony. Accompanying me were my wife, my eldest son and his fiancée at the time and now wife, and my other two sons. In my speech, I thanked the committee and all those who recognized the contribution of The First Five. Dock Rone and Arthur Dunning were also honored and were present and spoke. A-Club calls to Jerome Tucker went unanswered and Melvin Leverett passed away some years earlier. Dr. James Sanderson, I understand, spearheaded the efforts to recognize The First Five. The last time Dr. Sanderson and I spoke, he asked me if I would write a letter of nomination for Jerome Tucker to be voted on to become an honorary member of the A-Club. I gladly wrote the letter nominating Jerome and I also asked Dr. Sanderson to allow me to nominate Melvin Leverett, who is now deceased but was a part of The First Five.

I am not sure how many members were in attendance at the A-Club ceremony; 200 would be close to the actual number, I think. When it came my turn to come to the podium and speak, I suddenly noticed all the white men in the audience with gray hair—many of them my age or older. There was a spattering of black faces, but much younger black faces, which spoke to the relative recentness of the diversity of sports at Alabama. Thoughts raced through my mind of an earlier era when old white men represented the epitome of racial intolerance and social injustice; it *seemed* that that era had passed as everyone who greeted me appeared to be genuinely sincere in their well wishes.

As a type of an *aside*, let me share one other such instance. When I called a publisher at another publishing company regarding the publishing of this book, an older white woman answered the phone; she had been referred by a relative. When I heard her deep Southern dialect, I experienced the same déjà vu feeling that shook me at my A-Club induction. Isn't it funny how the mere sound of her voice and my mental image of an older white woman with a Southern drawl conjured up past negative experiences such that I did not continue further talks?

Notice that I used the word "seemed" when describing the racial intolerance and social injustice of a seemingly bygone era. With the 2016 presidential campaign season and the *selection* of Donald Trump to be president, the term "seemed" is very apropos at this writing. White folks made a statement and we, as black people, read the statement. We understand all too well the dog whistles and the clarion calls to hatred that have blossomed in this fertile soil. Moreover, we understand that fertile soil is not confined to the South. Although disappointed and hurt, I am at the same time heartened by the number of white people who did not vote for Donald Trump.

In my speech to the A-Club, I posed a question to a statement made by abolitionist and Unitarian minister, Theodore Parker circa mid-1800s, and later rephrased by Dr. Martin Luther King, Jr.: "The moral arc of the universe is long, but it bends towards justice." My question is, "Why must the moral arc of the universe be so long and why must it merely bend *towards* justice?" We have a moral duty to straighten out the arc by getting rid of the bend and to establish a flattened trajectory with all deliberate speed. Justice and morality should not have to always take a circuitous route.

My A-Club plaque reads: "In Recognition of Outstanding Contributions to Athletics, Andrew Pernell has been duly elected to Honorary Membership in the Alabama A-Club, University of Alabama, this 19th day of April, 2014." Now, that should quiet the arguments of the contrarians who questioned my legitimacy as an Alabama Crimson Tide football player and more importantly, the contrarians should be ashamed that I was not afforded a *real chance* to play in an official football game and had to settle for "honorary" membership. I hasten to add that I am eternally grateful to Dr. Sanderson, Coach Saban, and the others who sought to recognize and ameliorate a wrong committed and embraced in an era when racism was a way of life.

CHAPTER 11

The Revisionists, the Defenders, and the Judge

The tendency by some writers, reporters, and filmmakers to rewrite history, I think, is based on their reluctance to put their people's past malevolent behavior in a bad light. I believe that unadulterated truth is much more powerful and redeeming than contrived fiction. The early 19th century poet, William Cullen Bryant said that, "Truth crushed to earth shall rise again"; this utterance is more than just words—there is iron in those words.

Based on my experience with most of those people who interviewed me, wrote about me, or filmed me, I came away with the observation that *many* writers, reporters, and filmmakers *really* want to rewrite history—if not at a conscious level—certainly at a subconscious level. They want to not be uncomfortable and they want their audiences to not be uncomfortable in the hearing of the story. They want to put their heroes and *their* people in the best light—even reporters and filmmakers after having listened to my story—many of them put *their* spin on past events to which they were not a party or even an eyewitness.

Once upon a time at the University of Alabama, there lived one of the greatest sports legends of all times, Coach Paul "Bear" Bryant. As far as Alabama football fans are concerned, he was *the* greatest sports legend of all times. I have observed that several of those who interviewed me have attempted to make Bear Bryant out to be the greatest *integrationist* of all times when it came to the integration of sports at the University of Alabama.

Filmmaker Keith Dunnavant's Film

I found Keith Dunnavant's film, *Three Days at Foster*, very interesting, informative, and touching, but I was disappointed that Dunnavant did not include my less than flattering comments on Paul "Bear" Bryant regarding Bryant's lack of effort in integrating his team; however, Dunnavant *did* include the anecdotal piece regarding "Bear" Bryant offering Dock Rone a *ride* to football practice. And?

In an article (circa 2013), reporter Ray Glier wrote a special for *USA Today Sports*. Glier wrote this:

> Rone, who was standard size for a defensive lineman 45 years ago (185 pounds), was walking along University Boulevard one afternoon when Bryant pulled alongside in his car and asked him to get in. "He told me, 'I expect you to play for me this coming season,' Rone said."

We see here that Glier *repeats* the anecdote, first shared by Dunnavant, regarding Bear Bryant offering Dock Rone a ride. Is this the best evidence that can be presented that Bear Bryant was trying to integrate his team? This anecdotal evidence of Coach Bryant's intentions and efforts does not comport with the excerpts from Coach Bryant's 1970 *legal* deposition (see Appendix A). The deposition is replete with half-hearted recruitment efforts to integrate the team. The oft repeated refrain was that black athletes who were both athletically and academically qualified were as scarce as hens' teeth and that the ones that Bama really wanted, went elsewhere at the last minute.

White folks for whom my mother worked would oftentimes offer her a ride home at night after she had finished their housekeeping chores by day and babysat their children by night. What's the point of Dunnavant's comment about the offer of a ride? This inclusion by Dunnavant of the anecdote regarding Dock Rone spoke volumes as to the picture that Dunnavant was painting of Coach Bryant's stance on integration. Just because one gives a ride to someone is not necessarily indicative of where one's heart lies. In the 50s in the South, white bus drivers would pick-up black riders, but the blacks were relegated to the back of the bus. Are we clear?

During Jeff Sessions' Senate confirmation hearing (January 2017) to become the United States Attorney General, he found *two* Negro witnesses to testify how good Jeff treated *them*. One of the testifying Negroes, William Smith, said this, "After 20 years of knowing Sen. Sessions, I have not seen the slightest evidence of racism, because it does not exist. I know a racist when I see one, and I've seen more than one, and Jeff Sessions is not one."

History is replete with instances of Sessions' racism. His record of voting and policy making on relevant race issues speaks for itself. The American Civil Liberties Union (ACLU) rated Sessions at a 20% on civil rights issues. Sessions supports voter I. D. laws, stands against affirmative action, pushed for legislation to make English the only language of government services, and co-authored a bill aimed at eliminating a federal mandate that allows states to investigate ways of addressing the confinement of minorities disproportionately.

We as black people have always had some Negroes in our midst who would allow white folks to use them to speak on behalf of whites who had treated *them* (Negroes) good. Take Kanye West—-please! What about the masses of black folk who these racists, like Sessions, have negatively impacted their lives? Don't tell me about Bear Bryant offering Dock Rone a ride as proof for and evidence of his good will toward black athletes. That dog won't hunt either.

I have come to the conclusion that the agenda of many writers and other media people has already been established from the outset; they already know how the story will end. Becoming dismayed with the *re-telling* of my story by others from a third person perspective—acquired from secondary sources—I thought it my duty to report the story from the perspective of an eyewitness and participant. I am convinced that a primary source and account invariably trump a secondary source and account.

Filmmaker Keith Dunnavant's Spin

In Dunnavant's film *Three Days at Foster*, he seemed to imply that Bear Bryant was not a segregationist; he did not hate blacks—look—he offered a black player a ride. Reporters of all types must be objective in their reporting and storytelling. Oftentimes *stories* may not lead where the *reporter* or the filmmaker wants to go. I strongly suggest that if the story does not lead in that direction, don't go in that direction.

As a doctoral student, one of the first things that we learn is a concept called "situatedness." Our objectivity is tainted by the lens through which we view the world and it is unavoidable. Our situatedness has to do with our environments, our customs and traditions, our experiences, and our current situations. Dunnavant is a white Southerner, and as such, *his* story is viewed through *his* lens and his motivations; however, situatedness per se, does not the truth make.

Even though we may try to be as objective as possible, reporters and others must be aware of how their situatedness affects their reporting. A close second to situatedness is the duty to report alternative views right along with the main stream views being espoused. The duty to report alternative views, especially in a documentary, was viewed by me as *dereliction* of professional integrity. My view of Bear Bryant did not fit in with the narrative being constructed by Dunnavant.

I think that we could both straighten and shorten the moral arc if we would *allow* people to *handle* the truth. We want to play patty cake with white folks and spoon feed them so that they won't be too uncomfortable and that they will leave feeling good and that they will purchase our product. I submit that white folks can handle the truth—given a chance—albeit hard to handle; it's okay to be uncomfortable. Let's stop lying to people and sugar coating history and reality. My former pastor, Earnest Sanders, has many wise sayings; one of his sayings is that, "A lie travels fast, but the truth will catch up." It is what it is—it was what it was. Let's talk about it in hopes of really moving forward!

The Defenders

Over the years, sports writers and other commentators have conjured up scenarios that portray Coach Bryant as being a shrewd tactician, who always wanted blacks to play for him and he was *slowly* working the integration piece out behind the scenes. I have observed that this story has gained much traction.

One Bama fan and sports columnist, Kevin Scarbinsky, responded to an interview that I did for the *Birmingham News*, in which I said that Bear Bryant could have done much more than he did in bringing about integration to Bama. After proofing a draft of the interview, I asked the reporter not to print the draft in which he placed Coach Bryant in a much brighter light than I had; the reporter revised his draft in accordance with my original comments.

The fan, defending Bryant, said that it was *easy* to say that he could have done more—implying that Bryant had done what he could—or all that he could—given the *circumstances*. We must find the courage to do what is right in season and out of season. What we do *know* is that Coach Bryant sure didn't ruffle any feathers with the segregationist power structure—he didn't lay anything on the line in his so-called integration attempts. We know that Coach Bryant had power and influence; he diverted and helped a dually qualified black student-athlete football prospect to obtain a scholarship to a black university—not the University of Alabama.

To Mr. Scarbinsky, I say, "It is *easy* to say that Coach Bryant went as fast as he could, given the circumstances." The fan's comment has a lot to do with perspective or situatedness or relative location to the fire. Let me speak metaphorically for a moment in order to make my point. I would ask the fan to consider this: A man and his family are in a burning house and he has called the 9-1-1 operator and the operator informs him that the fire department is on the way; however, the fire truck driver does not turn on the siren for fear of waking the residents; the driver stops for each stop sign and stop light; the driver observes the posted speed limit all the way. I would say to the fan: If you and your family are in the burning house, there is a certain *urgency*—*"the fierce urgency of now."* You would no doubt want the fire rescue truck to sound the siren no matter if the residents are sleeping; you would want the driver to run the stop signs and stop lights and to exceed the posted speed limit.

I would say to Mr. Scarbinsky, who has come to Coach Bryant's defense regarding integration, it's *easy* to say go slow when *you* are not in the burning house and you are not concerned neither about the house nor the occupants. I believe that each of us is born with a sense of right and wrong and good and evil. Pastor Chelsea T. Pernell of Kingdom Keepers Church in Cleveland, Ohio, explains that God did not intend for man to know evil; man was not supposed to eat from the tree of the knowledge of good and evil (Genesis 2:17); however, man does know evil and wrong and evil and wrong have occupied the throne way too long.

Reporter Ray Glier, in his special for *USA Today Sports* had this to say:

> "The roles of Rone and others in the integration of the Alabama football program are featured in the documentary *Three Days at Foster*, released Monday. Bryant started a gradual push to integrate the program with Rone in 1967 while fierce segregationist George Wallace was governor of Alabama."

In the above paragraph, we notice that Glier gives credit to Coach Bryant for *initiating* the *gradual* push to integrate the mighty Crimson Tide. If you read Glier's earlier comments carefully, you will see that Coach Bryant did not initiate the contact with Dock Rone—Dock Rone initiated the contact by writing to Coach Bryant asking permission to walk-on. Two questions: (1) What evidence warranted Glier to conclude that this meeting was the impetus for integrating the Bama football program? (2) What was Glier's motive for interjecting the name and description of "fierce segregationist George Wallace" into the sentence? Was it to show what Coach Bryant was up against in his integration efforts and therefore *had* to go slow?

Man's knowledge of good and evil, coupled with man's free will, has led to man's penchant to do evil. No matter our upbringing, our environment, our times, I submit that we all know right from wrong. I further submit that in order to do wrong and to continue to do wrong, man must construct his own set of truisms that best fit his situation and that allow him to sleep at night; otherwise, he would suffer an extreme degree of cognitive dissonance—unless he was a sociopath. Let "…justice …roll down like waters and righteousness like a mighty stream" (Martin Luther King, Jr.; Amos 5:24).

Dr. Martin Luther King, Jr. wrote in his famous "Letter from a Birmingham Jail" (April 16, 1963) that "justice delayed too long is justice denied." In Dr. King's letter he said in part:

> "The Negro's great stumbling block in his stride toward freedom is not the White Citizen Council or the Klu Klux

Klan, but the white moderate, who is more devoted to "order" than justice, who prefers a negative peace, which is the absence of tension to a positive peace, which is the presence of justice…who paternalistically believes he can set the timetable for another man's freedom; who lives by a mythical concept of time and who constantly advises the Negro to wait for a 'convenient season.'"

I hasten to add that this letter was addressed to black ministers and Jewish leaders who had called Dr. King's civil rights activities "unwise and untimely." Even these two communities were foremost concerned with "order"—even though conditions for black people were atrocious. I have observed that placating the majority or those in power forces justice and what's right to take a back seat. We don't want to offend in any way, either the majority or the powerful. When others stand by silently and allow wrong and injustice to have their way, then wrong and injustice become the norm of the day.

Robert F. Kennedy said, "Few men are willing to brave the disapproval of their fellows, the censure of their colleagues, the wrath of their society. Moral courage is a scarcer commodity than bravery in battle or great intelligence. Yet it is the one essential, vital quality of those who seek to change a world which yields most painfully to change."

I remember another online comment in which one Bama fan came to the defense of Coach Bryant and the segregationist practices of keeping Bama lily white. The fan said that The First Five were not athletic standouts—as though that was sufficient reason to abridge our rights that were afforded to other similarly talented white athletes. I wondered how did he know that we were not athletic standouts; we lived in two different worlds and I would venture a guess that he did not know *any* black standouts. White players who were not athletic standouts have walked on at Bama and been accepted; some have made the team.

We just wanted to be treated like all other players. We should not have to be super men or super athletes or super students to be accepted by the football team or the school. Comments like this are pregnant with ignorance, defensiveness, and justification, as well as racism. Comments like those coming from the Bama fan are disingenuous at best.

Given the atrocious history of Alabama and race relations, one cannot mount a legitimate argument for denying blacks entrée into sports and white society in general. Segregation and the denial of individual rights based on skin color are both indefensible. Try as you might, you will end up identified as a racist. The preponderance of prima facie evidence is overwhelming that the above comments and arguments are without merit and are illegitimate. I was not surprised by the defender who posted the comments to *The Birmingham News* article—but my soul was *troubled*—so much so that I felt compelled to respond in depth and at length.

History Will Not Be the Only Judge

Oftentimes, when a people have mistreated another people—for whatever reason that seemed rational and plausible at the time—the mistreatment has proven to be frowned upon and abhorred over time. It seems clear to me that the best way to avoid being caught on the wrong side of history is to not mistreat a people. Think about it—when has the mistreatment of a people ever ended up placing the perpetrators in a good light when looking back from a historical perspective? How many heroes do we honor today because they mistreated people? Even in war, those who mistreat the enemy are not held in very high esteem by civilized society. Consider the chants of "Build That Wall" and the practice of locking up immigrant children in cages and permanently separating them from their families—how will this look on America's resume as "the greatest country in the world?"

What can we take away from this observation? Our present society grapples with populism, conservatism, and racism, but *history* will be the judge of the prudence of these ideas and their execution. I would posit that the judge would not hand down a sentence with which we could be proud. The times in which we live will become our past, just like slavery and segregation in their times. Many try to run away from that past; however, the deed has been done and there is *no* undoing.

Dr. Martin Luther King, Jr.—quoting Theodore Parker, the mid-1800s Unitarian minister and abolitionist—noted that "The moral arc of the universe is long but it bends toward justice." I submit to you that we, the people, can both shorten and straighten the moral arc if we just do what's right—no matter the *season*. I believe that each of us has an innate, God-given sense of what's morally right and what's morally wrong. Further, I think that when we *choose* to do wrong, we concoct a rationale for our wrong actions and thereby we are able to sleep at night. It seems, sadly, that oftentimes our environment and upbringing trump both our Christian or religious values and our innate values.

Moreover, it seems that our covenant with humanity should be that we will treat *everyone* as equals and seek fairness and justice in all our dealings with mankind. I have noticed that some Christians can take certain passages from the Bible and justify their own contrary beliefs and actions—even when the particular scriptures cited do not comport with the foundational tenets of Christianity. (For my brothers and sisters who are not of the Christian faith, my intent here is not to offend, but to expose the *Christian Nation* hypocrisy).

Many in our country like to have our country referred to *officially* as a "Christian Nation." Notice that I have placed "Christian Nation" in quotation marks to help point out the hypocrisy and dichotomous conduct between a "Christian Nation" and its observable actions and conduct. Maybe those who call ours a "Christian Nation" are invoking Romans 4:17 (KJV) and they merely "…calleth those things which be not as though they were." America champions and basks in high ideals, yet does not champion those who seek to execute and implement the high ideals.

"Mine eyes have seen the glory of the coming of the Lord; He is trampling out the vintage where the grapes of wrath are stored" (Julia Ward Howard's *Battle Hymn of the Republic*). These two lines align with

> Revelation 14:19-20: "So the angel swung his sickle to the earth and gathered the clusters from the vine of the earth, and threw them into the great wine press of the wrath of God"—the final judgment.

CHAPTER 12

Too Soon—Coach Bryant's Deposition

When speaking of heroes and sports icons—you'd better tread lightly. Fans, especially sports fans, do not like their heroes' and icons' image to be tarnished—they want to see them as perfect in every respect. I remember that U.S. Attorney General Bobby Kennedy said—"Don't make my brother bigger in death than he was in life"—referring to the remembrances and reflections contemporary with his brother John F. Kennedy's death. One can be great without being perfect.

The Afro-American Association of the University of Alabama brought a lawsuit against Coach Paul "Bear" Bryant. I was listed as one of the plaintiffs in the lawsuit. The suit was brought to basically *force* the University of Alabama and Coach Paul "Bear" Bryant to integrate the Crimson Tide football team. On July 8, 1970, Coach Bryant gave his 92-page deposition in the District Court of the United States for the Northern District of Alabama, Western Division. (Pertinent excerpts from the deposition are located in Appendix A).

What follows is one of the interchanges in the deposition (pages 12 and 13) with Atty. U. W. Clemon, Plaintiffs' attorney, questioning Coach Bryant:

Q: When did you begin recruiting blacks?

A: Well I guess three or four years ago we began looking in the State and this was prior to the time when they started blacks and whites playing one another. And our thinking was that any good ones came along, we certainly didn't want them to get away..."

Observe that in Coach Bryant's response, he basically stated that he began recruiting or at least looking for black athletes even *before* blacks and whites began playing together—a type of integration trailblazer some might say.

On pages 13 and 14 of the deposition, Atty. Clemon followed that response by asking Coach Bryant about steering an exceptional black athlete to a black college within the last three or four years. Coach Bryant explained that he assisted the player in getting a scholarship to a black school for the player's own good: [Coach Bryant talking about the conversation that he had with the black athlete's coach] "I told him if he comes up there we are going to treat him just like anybody else, but from one coach to another, if he was my kid, right now I believe it is a little too soon, I would direct him someplace else." Coach Bryant intimated that the player would be placed in harm's way if he played for Alabama because they would not only have to play in Starkville, Mississippi, and Oxford, Mississippi, but also in Tuscaloosa, Alabama.

Observe that in Coach Bryant's immediate prior response, he stated that he had been trying to recruit or at least look at black student-athletes for the last three or four years. In this latest statement in which Coach Bryant admitted steering a black athlete away from the University of Alabama to a black school within the last three or four years—and even helping him get a scholarship to the black school—Coach Bryant stated that "...it is a little too soon..." From actively recruiting or at least looking at black student athletes, to steering a black athlete of scholarship quality to a black school, makes the two statements taken together hard to swallow or incongruous at best. As former President Bill Clinton once said, "That dog won't hunt."

Why was it *too soon* for right and justice and fair play? Why the need to wait? It's easier to *wait* when it's not your house that is on fire. This is a sad commentary on Starkville and Oxford and Tuscaloosa—it is part of the history of these people; the deed has been done, there is no undoing.

Remember me sharing with you the story about the University of Alabama registrar who firmly suggested that I go elsewhere (anywhere else) out of concern for my happiness? This is the incident that I am reminded of when I read in Coach Bear Bryant's deposition that he not only directed an academically and athletically qualified, star black football player to an all-black college, but he *helped* this qualified star football player *obtain* a football scholarship at the all-black college. What power and influence—used to maintain the status quo!

The Academically Unqualified Myth Dispelled

In his deposition, Bear Bryant testified that he tried to recruit black players on many previous occasions, but said that he could find only a rare few who were academically qualified as well as athletically qualified. And wouldn't you know it, those dually qualified black football players signed elsewhere! Coach Bryant and others of his era would always hide behind "not academically" qualified, feeding into the stereotype that all blacks were academically challenged and thus, unable to meet the white man's standards; hence, blacks are inferior.

It is my opinion, based on facts, observation, and experience, that in our society—not just the South—race trumps everything—even winning. (In my soon to be released book, *A Matter of Race*, I discuss how race is still the center pole in the tent that covers our society; race is the cornerstone of day-to-day life in America).

Go North Young Black Man, Go North

How many Alabama blacks and other Southern black athletes during those times were forced to take their talents north of the Mason-Dixon Line? Blacks did not just recently begin to be athletically gifted or academically qualified. I submit to you that there is no *good* argument to support segregationist practices as were embraced by so many institutions. I have to admit, though, that there are many *dumb* arguments that are steeped in denial of past wrongs and injustice that are offered to settle the conscience of the segregationists.

The term "segregationist" is pretty much a euphemism, which works to disguise all the ugliness that is embodied therein: racism, hatred, subjugation, mistreatment, abridgement, nullification, subterfuge, deception, arrogance, etc. Suppose that we could not use the term "segregation" in our speaking, but instead of saying the word, we had to describe "segregation" in its fullest sense, using the above terms. Would that even make a difference?

Remember when I related earlier that the University of Alabama registrar told me that my grades were not on a par with the rest of the students and that he thought that I would be happier somewhere else? Well, they were good enough for me to be admitted *and* I graduated from the University of Alabama in four years. I wasn't a super student, but Bama is not populated by just super students and super athletes.

Red "Staters"

Today, some 53 years later, we observe that Alabama is a glowing politically and socially "red" state—still holding onto antiquated ideas, attitudes, and politicians that belong to a bygone era. I note that not all Alabamians have "red" state thinking, but there are enough of them to place the state into a solid "red" state category, along with Mississippi, Georgia, Louisiana, Texas, and the like. I would be remiss if I didn't add Michigan, Minnesota, Wisconsin, and my adopted state, Ohio.

Saying that Alabama is a "red" state further identifies Alabama as a state that is opposed to the principles of civil rights for all. Observe that the state of Alabama, and other Southern states, in response to the Civil Rights Movement, bolted to the Republican Party to find comfort and refuge *away from* those espousing "liberty and justice for all." So you see, it is a hard argument to defend against past deeds that were done in this red state social context. I submit to you that the "Red State" moniker that Alabama and other like states carry, is akin to the "segregation" label in its euphemistic garb. Not only are "Red State" and "segregation" convenient euphemisms, but they are siblings—fathered by racism.

Just as I began to close out this memoir, I read a disturbing and revealing article concerning and affirming many of the points that I have striven to make in this narrative. The article was titled, "Miranda's Rebellion," written by Stephanie McCrummen of the *Washington Post*, and was posted online on March 1, 2020.

The writer talks about two friends, who share their innermost thoughts with each other and to the exclusion of others; the friends are Miranda and

Liz. Through the sharing of their private conversations, the writer—without commentary—allows their words to describe many of the manifestations of racism and the Trump factor that is pervasive in rural, and sometimes not so rural places, as Columbus, Georgia, even as you read this. Columbus, Georgia, has a population of about 200,000 that is 45% black (2019) and 44% white (2019) and is located in west central Georgia.

Miranda and Liz are two suburban white women who have found it increasingly harder to live a lie and a lifestyle with which they do not agree. Liz is more active than Miranda in addressing and disagreeing with the established norms and mores of their city. Miranda grapples with her innate feelings of right and wrong regarding race and Trump; her sociopolitical environment has a stifling grip on her expressions of disagreement with the status quo, the hypocrisy, and the perpetuation of the lingering for a bygone era.

The article opens a window into how rural Southern white folks think and behave and what they say and think amongst themselves about black people. This opening is provided by a rural Southern white woman. These white folks are the "Deplorables" who Hillary was referring to when she ran for president in 2016. The Deplorables: They don't read; they don't think critically; they don't want to share America with "others"; they don't want any alternative view or behavior.

The difference between Miranda and Liz is that, Miranda lacks courage—and that is really eating at her. One of my slogans is: "Nothing binds so tightly as the chains that we put on ourselves." A corollary to that slogan would be: "Nothing binds so tightly as the fear of the reactions of our fellows when we are not in lock step on matters of commonly held sociopolitical beliefs and notions."

There have been other whites, albeit a very few, who venture to voice publicly what whites really feel, think, and say about black people. Author David Billings in his book, *Deep Denial: The Persistency of White Supremacy in United States History and Life*, spills the beans. He is a born and raised white Southerner from Arkansas and Mississippi. In the magazine, *The New Social Worker*, reporter Sandra Bernabei interviews Billings; she, in part, records this:

Bernabei: Let's begin with some definitions. It's hard to have a conversation about racism without defining it first.

Billings: Absolutely correct. Let me lay out a few key definitions here. First, **racism.** As we define it at the People's Institute where I work, racism is much more than a negative feeling about someone with different skin color. That emotion is called prejudice. Racism is race prejudice plus *power.* In the United States, **racism is structural.** It is rooted in our country's history. Since early colonial days, white people have had the power to establish laws, structures, cultural mores based on our biased attitudes and beliefs about people of color. That means that even today, although legal discrimination is outlawed, white people continue to have dominant structural power. Despite what we may believe as individuals, our institutions are built with prejudice in favor of white people and against people of color.

The second key definition is **antiracism.** To be antiracist is to believe that all people can reach their full potential as humans only when our society transforms its institutions so they are no longer biased in favor of white people. **Undoing** racism, then, requires us to act! It means understanding how this country's history impacts us both consciously and unconsciously, and then working to end structural racism in all our institutions.

The Billings book, especially the interview excerpts, validates much of what I have been penning in this book. Coming from a red state—a deep South born and raised white man—his words carry much weight in that they expose what has been hidden and what has been denied deeply and consistently. Some whites may read my work and argue (deny) the truth of my assertions and assessments. Having heard from such a man who is "in the room" when whites speak and act, makes denial much less plausible. A lie travels fast, but the truth catches up (Rev. Ernest Sanders).

If I was a white person—especially a Southerner—and I did not want any of my comments to appear insensitive or racist, I would just keep my mouth shut when it comes to speaking on race *defensively*; it's like a person coming from a family of child molesters speaking sympathetically and empathetically in defense of child molesters. For fear of being *suspected* of being a child molester too, such person would be wise to keep his/her mouth shut.

In March, 2016, David Duke, Grand Master of the Klu Klux Klan, endorsed Donald Trump for President of the United States. It is not a stretch to say that the values, antics, and positions of Donald Trump are aligned with those of the Klu Klux Klan enough such that David Duke endorsed Trump. What does this say about those (Red Staters—and others) who support Donald Trump? Birds of a feather flock together.

Notice that Trump has not come right out and said "Nigger," but the code words and the dog whistles that spew from his mouth are understood by white folks. This is why they rally around him—no matter what he says or does. Some happenings which we are aware of at this writing: (1) Housing discrimination against blacks in New York, (2) The Central Park Five persecution of five innocent black youth, (3) failure to pay his vendors, (4) the Access Hollywood tape, (5) adultery: extramarital affairs over marriage to three wives, (6) secret hush money pay-offs to Stormy Daniels and Karen McDougal, (7) being a prolific liar, etc. As long as the message can be disseminated that you are against the welfare of black people and other non-white people, then it doesn't matter what else you say or how you behave.

Donald Trump was recently impeached by the U. S. House of Representatives. Senate Republicans *refused* to convict him, even though the evidence against Trump was overwhelming. Republican senators were afraid of being "Trumped" and "primaried." These two terms are twins; "Trumped" means being the recipient of Trumps vindictiveness and "primaried" means being the recipient of Trump's influence with his "Deplorables."

The Deplorables are on Trump's team—this is a significant observation. Hillary got it right; the Deplorables used the term to generate even more ire to bolster their arguments against Hillary Clinton. It's akin to being a fan of a particular team; no matter how bad the team performs year-in and year-out, the fans stick with the team. They stick to him like glue and when he marches into hell, maybe they will still be stuck to him.

What is the glue that holds the Trump team together? Racism! One might characterize this phenomenon as "tribalism" or some other euphemistic term; however, we as black people see through the charade—even though white, mainstream news reporters buy into the triabalism construct. "Tribalism" isn't even in the standard dictionaries, but it has made its way into the online vernacular recently. How convenient to construct a new, more euphemistic term to describe racism; *racism* is such a harsh word.

To describe hatred against another race as "tribalism" is much, much more palatable than to describe the hatred as "racism"—isn't it? However, tribalism, by definition, does not embody *hate* for another race—just *love* of one's own race or group. Tribalism does not carry the baggage of hate for non-tribal people. As I think about this notion of *tribalism*, I see that the current use of the term is not appropriate for the attitudes and behaviors that the term is meant to capture. Tribes are relatively small groups of homogenous people; however, racism is nationwide and I submit that the term *racism* is more fitting.

Experientially, I recognize that people who were once called racists have taken on a more euphemistic and shielding moniker—they have begun to use the alias "conservatives." I was reading recently how the historically solid Democratic South evolved very quickly into the Republican South in conjunction with the passage of federal Civil Rights legislation in the 1960s. To be clear, Civil Rights legislation helped black people in various ways because black people needed help in various ways—mainly due to the bi-fold legacy and vestiges of slavery and its progeny—segregation and discrimination.

As of this penning (March 20, 2020), the Corona Virus is spreading like wild fire in America and across the world; lives and livelihoods are being lost or at least—diminished. Trump's initial response to the virus was that this thing was a "Democratic hoax" and that it was "fake news" and it would be over soon.

I have a couple of questions: (1) How much time did we lose during the "Democratic hoax" and "fake news" phase before Trump took any action? (2) Will the Trump supporters remain glued to him as they bury their loved ones? We all knew that Trump was not equipped intellectually or mentally to be the head of this country (or any other country); we knew that he was too incompetent to handle the job. When this pandemic is over, no matter the ravages to the country, I bet that Trump's racist supporters will still be stuck to him like Crazy Glue. You see, sadly, race trumps everything in this country.

Profiles in Lack of Courage

I make an argument in this book that Coach Paul "Bear" Bryant could have used his enormous power and considerable influence to bring about desegregation, not only at the University of Alabama, but elsewhere, because of the domino effect. I posit that integrating the Crimson Tide would have paved the way for desegregation over a broader landscape than just Bama football and Bama sports. Other coaches and university heads would have found a leader in Coach Bryant and would have been less hesitant in integrating their teams and universities. Oftentimes, it only takes *one* to get the ball rolling.

If Alabama had started winning and dominating with black athletes in that era—as they do now—then there would have been added pressure on other teams to integrate their squads also. I know that coaches and fans love to win and that other colleges would not be outdone by Alabama. The *St. Petersburg Times* article adds weight to my argument. The article continued by explaining why protests had been basically nonexistent in regards to The First Five black players, saying "...anyone in Alabama, including ex-Gov. George Wallace, hesitates before criticizing the undefeated Crimson Tide and its legendary coach, Paul (Bear) Bryant." My sentiment here is summed up by former President John F. Kennedy, "To those whom much is given, much is expected."

Mr. "Gingerly"

I made comments on the *Back Story* radio podcast on January 12, 2013, regarding Coach Bryant and his relatively slow pace in integrating the Crimson Tide, and one caller/writer took issue those comments. I will refer to him as Mr. "Gingerly." Mr. Gingerly's basic argument is that Bear Bryant went as fast as he could, given the Alabama climate of the times. Mr. Gingerly informs us that his dad viewed Bear Bryant as a "god;" this statement adds shoulders to my assertion that given Coach Bryant's god-like stature, he could have and should have done more sooner and I posit that Coach Bryant would have been successful in his efforts.

I see that by Mr. Gingerly's comments that he is a supporter of the notion that the moral arc of the universe is long. People like him, who are afraid to upset the status quo, greatly contribute to the length of the moral arc. Mr. Gingerly seems to be of the opinion that doing right has its season. I submit to Mr. Gingerly and the world, that doing right is *always* in season. Mr. Gingerly ends his comments by stating that, "Does that mean he [Bear Bryant] could have been stronger? Well, I guess but it must have been hard to live in those shoes." Poor Bear Bryant.

One more comment about Mr. Gingerly and others of his ilk, who take sides with the status quo and those in power. No attention or regard is paid to the *victims* who suffer under the status quo—Mr. Gingerly did not mention the victims even one time. Is empathy missing in this contrived system of segregation and injustice that inures only to the benefit of whites? When one has secured one's own freedom, comfort, and security, one may not be very eager for others to secure theirs. Is this the embodiment of "conservatism"?

The 1970 Deposition

For Mr. Gingerly and others of a like persuasion, consider the following:

I have just finished reading Coach Bryant's 95-page deposition concerning a law suit brought against the coach by the University of Alabama's Afro American Association in July, 1970. The deposition in sum revealed that the University of Alabama in the '60s had recruited black high school star-caliber athletes with half-hearted efforts at best. Toward the end of the '60s, Bama's black recruiting efforts increased somewhat.

Coach Bryant proffered, in defense of the lack of black football players on the Crimson Tide football team that (1) the black players who Bama offered scholarships to went elsewhere at the last minute, and (2) the black players who they were prepared to offer scholarships had poor grades for the most part and/or could not achieve a score of at least 17 on the ACT. Notice the use of the language, "...could not achieve..." Did this mean that achieving at least a 17 on the ACT for blacks was an impossibility? I am curious as to how Alabama subsequently found *so many* fine qualified black football players and other black athletes that had good grades *and* scored 17 or better on the ACT? Had they been looking in all the wrong places when they searched the countryside?

Power and Influence Unused

What good is power and influence if it is not used? I have said elsewhere and at other times that Coach Bryant could have done more than he did to integrate his football team *sooner*. The people of Alabama *worshipped* him and many still do posthumously. Where was courage when the situation and justice demanded courage? Absent!

I believe that Coach Bryant's power and influence and his voice could have made a difference in the integration of sports, not only in Alabama, but throughout the South and the nation. I do not limit my statement to Alabama and the South, because I understand that many colleges and universities throughout the country had their own struggles with desegregation. I view this country as down South and up South, which may be a more apropos view than down South and up North when drawing a distinction regarding racism; there is less of a sociopolitical distinction than we would like to believe—check your red and blue states map—a distinction without a difference.

Powerful and influential people—such as Coach Bryant—could have made a difference during those times when courage was needed. People like Coach Bryant knew that it was not right or just to deny people based solely on their color, but they remained quiet and acquiescent. I submit that that is why the moral arc of the universe is so long. But power is derived from the people and is contingent on their continued consent. Powerful people are oftentimes afraid—lack of courage—to speak out because of this dynamic and their dependency on public approval to remain in power and adoration.

In regards to power and influence, here is what attorney, turned sports writer, Thomas Hauser, wrote on the matter in an article "A Disillusioning Conversation with The Great Bear Bryant, which appeared in *The Sporting News:*

> Bryant epitomized an era when college football coaches were regarded as gods. Men like Bud Wilkinson (Oklahoma),

Woody Hayes (Ohio State), Bob Devaney (Nebraska), Darrell Royal (Texas) and Ara Parseghian (Notre Dame) were larger-than-life figures who could do no wrong in the eyes of their supporters. They were admired and adored the way military generals who lead troops into battle were venerated by previous generations of Americans.

The widespread assumption was that, had Bryant chosen to run for governor of Alabama in the 1970s, he would have been elected.

What I am about to relate is an aside, but I thought it relevant to include here. Remember Sam Gellerstedt, the football player who came to me in private in the locker room? Well, the title of Thomas Hauser's article, "A Disillusioning Conversation with The Great Bear Bryant," was basically about Sam Gellerstedt. In an autobiography of Coach Bryant, published by Little, Brown, Coach Bryant had said some less than flattering things about Sam and—through inference from Bryant's comments—Sam's family also. Sam sued and won a sizeable settlement.

I will not share the details because I count Sam as a caring and important human being in my life. Sam left the University of Alabama in 1968, after earning first team All-American recognition. He continued his successful football career at the University of Tampa. Also, I will not share the details about less than flattering comments about Coach Bryant made by Hauser because it does nothing to add to my point about power and influence.

Hauser closes his article with, "Our sports gods aren't always what we think they are and want them to be." This comment really sums up my point regarding Coach Bryant's lack of courage in doing more to integrate his team. A great coach—undisputed! A great integrationist—nope.

Cute Catchy Phrases

Also, in the HBO film *Breaking the Huddle*, I watched and heard a black *Birmingham World* sports columnist say that Paul Bear Bryant did more for integration of sports than Dr. Martin Luther King, Jr. did in twenty years—a big fat lie. Statements like this are unfortunate, uninformed, untrue, and minimize the *work* that civil rights heroes like Dr. King and others like him did in a quest for civil rights, justice, and integration. This comment by one of our black brothers highlights his ignorance and insensitivity to the intense struggle that was fought so close to home. If he is too young to remember, all he has to do is to ask his mother and father about how much Bear Bryant did for integration and how that made their life better.

The *forced* integration of the Bama football team related to sports specifically—not to the broader race-related problems faced by blacks, which the narrow-minded and short-sighted sports columnist evidently did not consider. The phrase "did more for integration than..." is catchy, though.

People like catchy phrases whether they be worthwhile or true or not. I remember a comment made during those early days that went something like this: "Bear Bryant would play a purple alligator if he thought it would help him win." The meaning here is that Bear Bryant would play *anybody* if he thought the person could help him win—not so. Sounds good, though. The truth is, the purple alligator would have a better chance at being recruited by Bear Bryant than a black, qualified star football player during those early days. I am quite sure though, that the purple alligator would have been better received by Alabamians than the black football player during those times.

The work and courage of such pioneers as Autherine Lucy in 1956 and Vivian Malone and James Hood in 1963, paved the way for others—like The First Five in 1967—to set the ball in motion for the eventual integration of the University of Alabama sports teams. Without this prodding, the Crimson Tide might still be lily white or it would have been lily white for a much longer time than it was. The birth of an Autherine Lucy or a Vivian Malone or a James Hood or The First Five is a product of segregation and all of its egregious attendants.

Negroes Both Academically and Athletically Qualified Impossible to Find?

Within the same *St. Petersburg Times* article of April 13, 1967, the writer reports that Alabama coaches had been "searching the Alabama countryside for months to find a Negro youth who can maintain grades and play football well enough to be awarded a scholarship." It makes you wonder where had other college coaches—outside of the south— been searching when they found a lot of Negroes who maintained grades and played well enough to start and star for their teams? Once again, the "banana in the tailpipe" trick worked with our white brothers and sisters. Where was the *critical* reporting? There is a huge difference between *simple* reporting and *critical* reporting.

How could the *St. Petersburg Times* reporter be so wantonly gullible? Given Alabama's history up to that time, what would make him believe that Crimson Tide coaches had been "searching the Alabama countryside…" high and low? From whom did he get this bogus information? Where was critical thinking or critical reporting?

Many accounts of The First Five record that four of The First Five, with the exception of Dock Rone, were held out of practice the first week because our academic standing had to be checked out. We were already well into our freshman year—we were not trying to *enroll*—our grades were good and our ACT scores were good as well. I, and Arthur Dunning included, have no recollection of being required by the team to sit out at all.

Coach Bryant passed away on January 26, 1983, of a massive heart attack in Tuscaloosa, Alabama. In an article by reporter Michael Wilbon in *The Washington Post* (January 29, 1983), Wilbon gives his readers a vivid picture of the funeral. Wilbon describes the extraordinary size of the procession and service for this extraordinary man: 400 cars and 8,000 mourners. He gives us a picture of the travel route from Tuscaloosa to Birmingham—about 51 miles—where at almost every overpass, crowds were gathered, holding up banners and placards with expressions of love.

Wilbon quoted the words on several signs seen in the crowds. Wilbon writes this about one such sign: "In a black section of Bessemer, youngsters held a sign that read, 'Thanks for the Memories, Bear.'" Wilbon concluded his article with several paragraphs devoted to comments by a former black player, Kelvin Croom (who I met at the 2011 Symposium on race and consider a nice guy):

> "One thing that disturbs me the most is that Coach Bryant died with some black people putting him down.
>
> He was a father to me as much as any white player. He hired my brother (Sylvester) as an assistant.

In 1975, I played as a freshman but I hurt my knee real badly. The doctors cleared me to play, but Coach Bryant told me I would never play again. He kept me on scholarship when he didn't have to, and I helped him recruit. He inspired us (black players) to make something of ourselves.

The next comment is *very* revealing:

If Coach Bryant ever was (a racist) he changed his mind. He told the team once that he was brought up a certain way and didn't know any better. But he said he had to change quickly. And he did because his door was always open, and I went in many times."

Note this: Bryant was born in a tiny rural town called Moro Bottom, Arkansas—a town so small that it wasn't even on the map when Bryant was born. The family was so poor that other town's people made fun of the Bryants. I wonder what was the "certain way" that Bryant was referencing when he was talking about how he was "brought up". It appears that this dirt poor Moro Bottom family and town had time to bring up Bryant in a "certain way." Moreover, bringing up a child in a certain way would always give the poorest of the poor someone to look down on and thereby more easily accept their own station in life.

I have a few questions—which can be taken as rhetorical—regarding the above comments. The first is, why did Wilbon, a black reporter, cite the young *black* crowd in Bessemer? What point was he making? The second question is why didn't Wilbon provide the socio-historical context for Croom's glowing assessment of Bear Bryant? Maybe the intent of Wilbon's writing this article was to convey *only* fond remembrances of the Bear and not deal with the contextual backstory, given the customary respect given the deceased during funeral proceedings; I accept that.

Croom's remarks about the thing that disturbed him the most about black people and Croom's reluctance to believe that Coach Bryant was a racist are important pieces taken in combination. I hasten to add that *I* did not call Coach Bryant a *racist* or even bring up the term. Kelvin Croom, a black man, is disturbed *the most* by "some black people putting him down." Do some black people have any reason to put him down? If Coach Bryant treated *him* good and *his* brother good, then does this personal testimony regarding the post-1974 Bryant, be the view that everyone else should hold of Coach Bryant?

A final comment regarding Croom's assessment of Coach Bryant as a person. In the context of being racist, Croom says "if" Coach Bryant was ever a racist, he changed. "If" Coach Bryant was a racist, *when* did he change? I wonder if Croom would be disturbed even more by some white people putting down Coach Bryant—like sports reporter Thomas Hauser; according to Croom, Coach Bryant admitted that, based on his upbringing, "he didn't know any better." But he "had to *change* quickly." I believe that Coach Bryant *changed*.

It was a bit ironic that Coach Bryant's funeral procession passed by my automobile detail shop in Powderly on Jefferson Avenue S. W. en route to Elmwood Cemetery in Birmingham. I saw the long procession as it passed my shop; I paused very briefly. I don't remember if I was ambivalent toward the funeral procession or if I was numb to it; I harbored no ill feelings nor cherished any fond memories.

CHAPTER 13

Black and White in Crimson

I was invited down to Tuscaloosa to participate in a symposium: "Black and White in Crimson – A Symposium on Race and Sports," sponsored by the University of Alabama's History Department's Friends of History. The symposium was held over a two-day period, November 3– 4, 2011, in the Bryant Conference Center. Professor Andrew Doyle of Winthrop University was the keynote speaker for the first day and Professor John David Briley of East Tennessee University was the panel moderator for the second day.

As I was driving around on campus trying to find the hotel where my family and I would be staying overnight for the second day of the symposium, I saw a young white, female student carrying books. I stopped the car and asked her for the hotel location. She addressed me as "Sir" in her response to me; she was very cordial and polite. I was *completely* amazed in that she addressed me as "Sir." I had not been to the Tuscaloosa campus since I graduated in August 1970; I was taken aback—in a good way.

During those days when I was a student, I would have never been addressed as such or I wouldn't have been responded to at all. I had been *conditioned* to expect rudeness and meanness and inhospitable behavior. I was pleasantly surprised and I hoped that this interchange was a harbinger of experiences to come.

The Friends of History had invited blacks who were "the first" in several sports categories at Alabama to be panelists. In attendance was the first black basketball player, the first black cheerleader, the first head coach to coach a black basketball player, the first black quarterback, and so on. All of the other panelists, who came several years later than I, shared experiences that were less caustic than the experiences that I shared. I observed that there is a difference in treatment *and* experience when one is an *intruder* as opposed to one who is an *invitee*.

During the symposium, I shared with the audience some of my negative experiences during my years with the team. I gave *my* assessment of former Coach Mal Moore because my experience with him stuck with me all those years, but I did not divulge his name when I spoke about him; however, former University of Alabama quarterback and fellow panelist, Walter Lewis, who is black, discussed how hard Coach Moore was on him. Walter said that Coach Moore would, on occasion, "kick" him at practice when he messed up.

Walter played at the University in 1980; my experiences with Coach Moore were during the years 1967-1968, 12 or 13 years earlier. When Walter named Coach Moore as the one who kicked him, I blurted out, "Yeah, that's the same coach who I was talking about." I was excited about the exposure of Coach Moore and his actions, but I was appalled that these kicking incidents could occur as late as 1980 at the University of Alabama.

My intent at that symposium was to conceal Coach Moore's name; however, his name was placed on the table when Walter mentioned his name in a similar context. Walter was relaying his experiences with a certain degree of fondness—it seemed to me—maybe the kicking was taken out of context. But I was thinking how could this same coach be dishing out this kind of treatment to a black player almost 13 years later? Given Bama's history with segregation, how could a coach treat a black player in this fashion in *1980*? This was incredulous to me.

In a recent interview with Jerome Tucker—one of The First Five—I shared with him my sentiments regarding Mal Moore. In turn, Jerome shared with me that he also had had an encounter with Coach Moore that was in the same vein as mine. Jerome shared that he had mistakenly put on the wrong color practice jersey for that particular day; players were assigned different color jerseys based on that days printed practice team assignment. He said that Moore became so angry with him about putting on the wrong jersey that he made him run suicide drills. According to Jerome, Coach Bryant observed this action and immediately intervened in a chastising manner to Coach Moore; Jerome shared that Moore turned beet red after being called on the carpet by Coach Bryant for abusing Jerome—needlessly.

I take my hat off to Coach Bryant for his handling of this incident with Jerome. Remember, I never called Coach Bryant a racist; my main point is that he could have done more sooner, in terms of integrating the Crimson Tide. This response to the situation by Coach Bryant carries more weight to any argument that he was not a racist, than the offering of Dock Rone a ride to practice.

Jerome and I laughed as we recalled some of our shared and separate experiences at the University. It was not really *laughter* though, it was more like a guttural humph, humph, humph, as in "Can you believe that they actually treated us like that?" I think that the phone conversation with Jerome was a cathartic moment for both of us. As I write this book, I feel catharsis at work.

Coach Mal Moore – A Metamorphosis?

I knew some time ago that Coach Moore had risen to a level of prominence at the University of Alabama, but I didn't know whether he was still at the University and I didn't know that he had risen to the level of athletic director. I did not keep up with Alabama football because of the less than warm reception that I received at Alabama when I walked on to play football for the Tide. Treatment, such as I received, has long-lasting effects on people—like me—who have been mistreated.

A few days after I returned home to Ohio from the symposium in Tuscaloosa, I was sitting at my desk when my phone rang. It was a call from Athletic Director Mal Moore. He said that he had talked to Walter Lewis and Walter had suggested that he give me a call.

We exchanged cordial greetings at the beginning of the phone conversation. Evidently Walter had told Coach Moore what I had said regarding how he treated me, but actually, Walter is the one who placed his *name* with the picture that Coach Moore had painted. Athletic Director Moore told me that he did not know that I felt that way and continued by saying that we were both young and that he had a lot of pressure on him.

I didn't ask Athletic Director Moore regarding the kind of pressure or the *source* of the pressure. Maybe the pressure that he felt was professional and due to his trying to be an outstanding coach, or maybe the pressure that he felt derived from external sources that he wanted to please, or maybe the pressure was internally grown and he was just showing who he was or who he had learned to be—I don't know. Whatever the source of the pressure, the pressure was applied to me and I suspect, others.

Moore stated that he wished that I had called him or come to see him earlier and I told him, in light of the treatment 44 years ago, I was reluctant to make contact because I didn't know how I would be *received this time*. Some actions leave lasting impressions. I had no reason to believe that he had changed to the point where we could talk about those days.

Moore ended the call by inviting me down to chat with him the next time that I was in Tuscaloosa. He never offered an explicit apology. I told him that I would come see him, but I was thinking at the time that it may not be good to visit with him since I was memorializing his name in this book and that he might read or hear of it before my visit with him. Moore passed away before we could once again meet face-to-face.

I wished I had gotten a chance to talk to him face-to-face so that I could explain how I felt and he could explain his actions. I am quite sure that an apology and forgiveness would have been appropriate after our dialogue. I think that I might have better understood the clutches of segregation and the hold that tradition had on him.

I will never get a chance to talk to him regarding the *early* days. I am quite certain that Mal Moore, when he was a young assistant coach, never imagined that he would rise to be athletic director at the University of Alabama one day, and I am even more certain that he never imagined that the Crimson Tide football teams would become predominantly *lily* black on his watch.

I don't think that people are born haters, but that many of them are born into environments where tradition and hate trump right and justice. I might have understood better after meeting with Mal Moore, but understanding does not equal justification. Why does the arc of the moral universe have to be so long? Why can't justice and right be our modus operandi?

For the record, I acknowledge that people can change. The Clear Lake, Texas, mother who drowned her five children in the bathtub in 2001, later petitioned the court to allow her out of her mental institution to attend church on Sundays. Her lawyer argued that she had *changed*. She may well have changed, but the act had been done; her five children were dead, the deed cannot be undone.

Some may say that Mal Moore is not here to tell his side of this story and that's not fair. Let me just leave the matter like this: My above comments represent *my* experiences with Mal Moore, the assistant coach, during the period 1967–1968. Even if he was here, I still experienced what I experienced.

Some may differ with my assessment of Moore, but this is *my* assessment based on *my* experience—this is *my* truth! I pray that he did change his heart and his attitude. Seems like it takes Southerners longer than most to accept change and *others*. As I understand it, there is no white heaven and black heaven.

Level of Education – No Affect on Racism

During my research, I saw that Mal Moore had earned a degree in sociology; I am one course away from a degree in sociology myself. I have taken many sociology courses and I was of the opinion that people who are learned in sociology are more likely to be more tolerant and less prejudiced against people who are different from them. I also learned in one of my sociology classes that, contrary to popular belief at the time, *level* of educational attainment does not necessarily make one less prejudiced, but it gives one a way to express one's prejudices in more dignified and eloquent ways, although Mal Moore's expressions were neither dignified nor eloquent in the early days.

We write history while we live, not when we are dead; therefore, let us now endeavor to write the kind of history that we want to be told about us when we are dead. What was done was done and cannot be undone by a gloss over. It is what it is.

CHAPTER 14

"Somebody Does Remember"

One night in 2009, I was channel surfing and came across a television program already in progress. It was HBO's sports documentary *Breaking the Huddle*. The program focused on the integration of sports at Southern colleges and universities. Dick Heller, long time sports columnist for the *Washington Times*, after viewing the HBO documentary, wrote in the newspaper, *DC*, "Young viewers will find it hard to understand why the issue of whites and blacks attending school together was such a volatile issue in the South over five decades ago. An *old* viewer like me still finds it hard to understand why the ruckus over blacks and whites together." I was also baffled about the necessity to separate people based on race; but not merely to segregate them, but to denigrate them, to subjugate them, to mistreat them.

Pulitzer Prize winning author, Isabel Wilkerson, in her book *Caste, The Origins of Our Discontents* (2020), sheds much needed light on my being "baffled." Her foundational work, which rips the covers off America's caste system, helped me understand the constructed structure upon which racism rests. Race, racism, and discrimination are all *intentional* and *devilish* in their execution, promulgation, and sustainability.

As I was watching the HBO documentary, I saw other black players being recognized for being the "first"—those that came much later than 1967. I was lamenting to myself the fact that "nobody remembered." I subsequently learned that I had missed the part of the documentary that showed a clip of me at practice—in uniform—at the University of Alabama—in *1967*! My wife came into the bedroom and began talking to me about some unrelated matter. I quickly drew her attention to the HBO program that I was watching and she began watching it with me; we sat in silence until the documentary was over.

At the end of the documentary, I said to my wife sadly, "Nobody remembers." For the very first time since the 1967 event and eight years of marriage, I shared my story in great detail—as one of the first five black football players who walked-on concurrently at Alabama, and as I learned some 47 years later—walked into history as pioneers in the integration of sports at Southern colleges and universities. The five of us just wanted to exercise our rights, as citizens of Alabama and the world, to play football for *our* school—*pioneering*, per se, was never even a conscious thought—not for me anyway. Can you blame us naïve teenagers for unwittingly putting our life on the line, in a very hostile environment, to not only attend the University of Alabama, but to play football? If it weren't for teenagers willing to take risks—oftentimes unwittingly—the civil rights movement of the 60s and its success may have occurred much later and much differently.

Career in Crisis – The Book That Changed My Life Course

In sharing my story with my wife, I recounted my experiences associated with being in the group of the first blacks to walk-on for football—or any other sport—at the University of Alabama. About a month later, my wife shared with me that after hearing my story, she was awakened by the Holy Spirit that very same night and the Holy Spirit said to her, "Somebody does remember." Being led by the Holy Spirit, she went to the upstairs office to the computer and keyed in, "University of Alabama Football Player Andrew Pernell" and a book popped up by author and Prof. John David Briley. The book is entitled, *Career in Crisis, Paul Bear Bryant and the 1971 Season of Change*. My name and facts about me appeared several times in the book's narrative.

Without reading about me and The First Five in *Career in Crisis*, I may have never set out to write this book or any book. Remarkably, John David Briley's book was very accurate concerning his narrative about me, even though he had been unable to interview me because he couldn't find me. In 2009, I learned that he had been attempting to contact me over a period of nine years to be interviewed for his book.

Finding me was very difficult because like so many other young Alabama black men and women graduating from high schools and colleges in Alabama during those times, I had to leave my native Alabama to find suitable employment in more progressive, tolerant states. Since graduating from the University of Alabama in 1970, I have lived in five states: Ohio, Georgia, California, Arizona, and Ohio—a second time.

Like I said, my wife did not share her Internet search findings until about a month after the airing of the HBO documentary; when she did share with me, she told me that her plan was to save that information until my January birthday in about two months, but she couldn't keep it any longer. My wife had, in hand, a copy of Professor Briley's book. When she finally shared her story with me of her search and findings and showed me the locations in the book where my name and information about me appeared—tears begin to flow unexpectedly and uncontrollably from my eyes. Oh, what a release! The news—to me—hit me like a ton of bricks. There was *some* recognition of The First Five and our contribution to integration in collegiate sports at Southern colleges and universities. The tears resulted from feelings of satisfaction, vindication, and validation.

Professor Briley, after the Alabama symposium on race, was very gracious in sending me a lot of news clippings from those times at Alabama. Reading the news clippings brought back many memories. I was totally unaware that such news was recorded of those events at Bama; I had never attempted research into those times. A couple of samplings of pertinent news clippings from those early days: The caption in an unnamed newspaper: *Crimson-White* Endorses Suit. The *Crimson-White* was the Bama student newspaper; its editorial comment was far ahead of the Southern thinking at that time—and maybe now also. The unnamed paper stated that the *Crimson-White* "…endorsed the complaint filed last week by the Afro American Association claiming discrimination in the recruitment of Negro athletes. The school paper noted that school officials have been quoted as saying the school searched for black athletes but added: "It is quite unrealistic to think that no blacks can be found to play football for the Crimson Tide."

I was happy that somebody did remember and recognized the efforts made and the price paid. I felt vindicated in that my time had not been wasted, even though it appeared that way to me for 42 years. I felt validated—that I had a valid claim to be recognized as a pioneer and football player for the mighty Crimson Tide. Long buried disappointments, repressed emotions, and silent anger—were all washed in my tears—but not washed away—as I realized that *somebody does remember*.

As I reflect, many years later, I may not have told my story with any regularity because I didn't want to take the scab off wounds that had not quite healed. For many years after Bama football, I *could not* cheer for the Crimson Tide. Acquaintances would sometimes ask me why I did not cheer for Alabama since I attended Alabama—my canned response was—"I just don't know." That response allowed me to not go into the sad details of "Why?" Vivian Malone had a similar reaction when sharing her story in her 2000 commencement speech at the University of Alabama. One cannot go quickly from being treated so cruelly to cheering for and with the same people who treated you so cruelly or who wanted to see you treated cruelly. The wounds are continuing to heal with the passage of time; as I observe the "changing of the guard," I am finally able to yell, "Roll Tide, Roll!"

Interviews and Speeches

I reside in Pepper Pike, Ohio, now—a suburb of Cleveland. I have received some notoriety relative to my experiences at the University of Alabama in the mid-60s. During the last several years, I have given talks at a couple of private schools in my area—Hawken School and The Ratner School. In November 2011, I participated in a symposium, sponsored by the History Department of the University of Alabama, on race: "Black and White in Crimson: A Symposium on Race and Sports." I have been interviewed and written about in *The Birmingham News* and a couple of Tuscaloosa (Alabama) magazines. I have given radio interviews on *Back Story* and *Life Obstacles*.

I was featured in Keith Dunnavant's film *Three Days at Foster*, and received ink in John David Briley's book *Career in Crisis: Paul Bear Bryant and the 1971 Season of Change*. In 2016, I was asked to share my story at my church during

Black History Month for the first time—*finally*. I was the keynote speaker at MEEK Academy in Cleveland, Ohio, in 2019 for the school's black history program and I was given the school's "Life Time Achievement Award."

At some of the places that I spoke, people seemed to be incredulous after hearing *my* story. Most of the people who interviewed me may have been incredulous too, when they asked, "It wasn't that bad, was it?" And, "It wasn't all of them, was it?" Several of those who have interviewed me—after listening to my story—ask in disbelief, the same questions. People don't want to really believe that many of the evils birthed out of segregation and Jim Crow laws produced such abhorrent behavior.

In one of my sociology classes in undergraduate school, I remember the statement: 'We do not abhor a thing because it is a crime; the thing is a crime because we abhor it." It seems fair to say that there was not sufficient abhorrence to prevent a lot of the deplorable actions (crimes) that were not only tolerated, but blessed by the citizenry in power at that time.

CHAPTER 15

The Changing of the Guard

On Saturday, November 5, 2011, after the symposium on race had ended, I wanted to see the old practice field where this journey all started, so I drove over with my wife and two of my sons. I wanted to see if the experience would usher back any memories of those early days. The practice field was a place where I spent many days in solitary confinement, on an island, surrounded by all white players and coaches.

So much had changed in regards to the practice field and the locker room facility in the 43 years since I last played there; it was a place that I did not recognize physically. I could not get close to or get a good look at the field because of the partitions in that area now; when I was playing, players could walk unabated onto the practice field and into the locker room. I lingered in the area for a while, but I could not get any vibe from bygone days—probably because I could not mentally visualize the field as it was in those days.

What was so poignant and memorable for me was that I saw a plethora of black players arriving to prepare for the "game of the century," Alabama vs. LSU. Many of the black players were dropped off by their girlfriends—I assume. It was so natural, it seemed, for them to walk freely into the locker room with no thought of the history that had preceded them. As I stood outside and they passed me by, they had no clue as to who they were passing.

On one level, I wanted them to know who I was. I am sure that they would have been in awe—well—maybe not. On another level, and the most important level, I was so happy that they could go about their business of game preparation *freely*, with no thought of whether they would be accepted or not by their white teammates or the fans or the coaches. I felt good! I felt good that I played a role in the freedom with which they moved about the locker room facility and the campus. That's the way it should have been long ago.

I was given two complimentary tickets to the game by the symposium committee, but there were four us. So I gave the tickets to our two sons to watch the game; my wife and I stayed in the car near the stadium, listening to the game on the radio. It was a beautiful day in Tuscaloosa. The air was filled with gaiety on this warm, bright, sunny, November day. Even though Alabama lost 6-9, it was such a beautiful day and such a feeling of contentment that we enjoyed.

I wonder sometimes how proponents of segregation feel now as they see how integral black athletes are to the success of the Bama football program. I wonder if their attitudes have changed with the changing times, and I also wonder if they have reflected on their positions and attitudes that they held or maybe still hold. With the prominence of the black athlete excelling at football at the University of Alabama and sports in general at the University of Alabama, as well as nationwide, the various reasons given—other than racism—for not recruiting black athletes from the outset have proven to be just a bunch of bull spit!

The Proliferation of Black Football Players in 2019

Recently, I was thinking about how well integrated Bama football and basketball teams are. The players are *well-received* and even idolized by some fans. There is not even a thought now that Bama has black players on its teams. What has changed since the 60s? Integration of sports is alive and well at the University of Alabama.

I was curious as to how many blacks were on the Alabama football roster in 2019, so I conducted my own research. I pulled up a team picture and sorted players by race—visually—as we are wont to do in this country. My research revealed that the 2019 University of Alabama football roster was comprised this way: (1) First team offense: 9 of the 11 (82%) players were black (or considered black by Southern standards). (2) Second team offense: 8 of the 11 (73%) players were black. (3) Starting defense: 11 of the 11 (100%) players were black. (4) Second team defense: 11 of the 11 (100%) players were black. My curiosity was answered in this calculation: 87% (39 out of 44) of the first and second team players, offense and defense, were black.

The statistics caused me to wonder further, where were all these academically qualified, athletically gifted blacks hiding when Coach Bear Bryant was "searching the countryside." Black athletes just didn't *suddenly* or *recently* acquire academic prowess and athletic giftedness. Could it be that many white coaches *knew* about the athletic skills of blacks, but they wanted to keep these gold nuggets separated from their white counterparts? Why must the moral arc of the universe be so long? And why does it have to be an "arc"? And why does it merely bend *towards* justice?

One could reasonably think that with all the love shown to the black players by white Alabamians, the state of Alabama would not still be such a *deep* red state. There seems to be little to no carry over to other sociopolitical areas. The tag "red state" carries a lot of negative connotations for and with black people. But, whites have historically shown love to black people who *performed* for and *entertained* them.

CHAPTER 16

Interview with Coach Pat Dye
of Auburn University

A few years ago, I interviewed former University of Alabama assistant coach and former head coach at Auburn University, Pat Dye. Coach Dye was an assistant coach at Bama during my tenure as a football player. When I talked to Coach Dye, he was serving as Assistant to the President of Auburn University. Coach Dye worked with the linemen—I think—and didn't remember me in particular; he did not remember which one of The First Five that I was, but he remembered The First Five as a whole. I felt comfortable in calling him because he was one of those coaches who didn't seem to mind us being around. As I have noted several times before, most black people have a knack for knowing *quickly* who is friend and who is foe—this knack is a key to survival in a hostile environment.

I wanted to interview Coach Dye and obtain his impressions of those early days at Bama. During the interview, Coach Dye initiated a discussion of the history of blacks in this country. Coach Dye *urged* me to include a section on the important contributions made by blacks in the development of this country. As he spoke, it was like fire shot up in his bones; it seemed as though he had wanted to tell somebody that for a long time. This statement was made in the context of the hundreds of years of free forced labor and underpaid labor of blacks.

The Case for Affirmative Action

To rally against affirmative action is to deny the long-lasting impact of slavery and segregation that inured to, and continues to be inured to the benefits of whites and their progeny for many generations and to the detriment of blacks and their progeny for many generations. How will we ever catch up when the playing field has been sanctioned as "level"? In connection with the Brando Starkey article on immigration, a Serbian worker proclaimed (circa 1924), "You know something about this country...Negroes never get a fair chance."

Fair play is screaming to be heard as we stand and remove our hats and wrap ourselves in the flag and bellow out "...the land of the free and the home of the brave." Fair play is screaming to be heard as we solemnly pledge allegiance to *our* flag; we end our pledge by proclaiming "...one nation under God. Indivisible, with *liberty* and *justice* for all." When will we ever realize our hypocrisy in regards to these words and begin to live up to our high ideals?

The incident that I am about to share with you happened in 1990, in Mesa, Arizona. I worked for a defense contractor as a cost/schedule control analyst. I was conducting a survey for my thesis. The title of my thesis was, "The Relationship Between Career Advancement and Educational Level at DEFCON." In addition to educational level, my thesis looked at other probable career advancement variables such as *race*, gender, height, weight, attractiveness, etc. I had cleared the use of my survey with my supervisor because I was conducting the survey among DEFCON employees on DEFCON time.

I passed out the surveys one morning to employees; by noon, all hell had broken loose—as they say. DEFCON security personnel approached me concerning my surveys and demanded that I give up the undistributed surveys. Security asked who had given me permission to conduct the survey and I told them that my supervisor had done so. When security questioned my supervisor regarding the same, he told them that he had given me permission, but that he wasn't aware of the nature of the questions.

DEFCON security, somehow determined which employees received the surveys; security confiscated the surveys from these employees; however, I was able to keep a small percentage of the completed surveys that had been returned to me. What was it that DEFCON did not want me to statistically find out about its company? Was career advancement based on any of the embarrassing variables—like race for example? I don't know. DEFCON was determined to not let me find that out.

Initially, I had disguised the name of the actual company for which I worked and the company that confiscated my surveys. The actual name of this company that acted in this way was McDonnell Douglas Helicopter Company in Mesa, Arizona. I thought, why should I shield them from their egregious behavior when I have given *credit*—exposure—to everyone else of whom I have written. I am 72 years old at this writing; I have no fear of any sort of retaliation; the truth stands on its own. The deed has been done, there is no undoing. Withholding the actual name was like fire shut up in my bones.

I discussed the matter with my thesis professor and he allowed me to use the limited number of completed surveys that I had been able to keep. Due to the forced small sample size, I was able to run a limited number of statistical tests; however, due to the limited sample size, I could not make a statistical representation about the population. My thesis advisor advised me to include in my thesis, the circumstances under which the survey was conducted and proceed with what I had gathered. I completed my thesis for my Master's Degree in Management, and graduated with the distinction of Magna Cum Laude.

I submit that those who fight affirmative action are in denial of the effects of past wrongs as well as the perpetuation of those wrongs. The opponents of affirmative action seem to want a level playing field *now* without making the playing field level; they fail to factor in the advantages that they have received just because they are white and all of their white fore parents who benefited from the systems of slavery and segregation. Some of the anti-affirmative action coalition will tell you that their parents did not have slaves and that they themselves did not discriminate against blacks. Neither did my parents nor I own slaves; however, my parents and I are burdened with the effects of slavery and its progeny. This type of anti-affirmative action rationale is shortsighted and selfish—not necessarily racist.

CHAPTER 17

I Can't Breathe

I completed writing this book several months ago; however, prior to going to print, the tragic murder of George Floyd occurred and the aftermath is ongoing. I discussed with my writing advisor, whether I should add a chapter in my book where I opine on those events. She thought that it would be a good idea and apropos in light of my fact-based claims, contentions, and assertions in my book—I agreed.

On May 25, 2020, 46-year old George Floyd—a black man—was murdered by Minneapolis policeman Derek Chauvin; three other officers aided and abetted in this callous broad daylight crime. The atrocious murder was caught on cell phone video by 17-year-old Darnella Frazier. Ms. Frazier, subsequently, was forced to move out of her house to an undisclosed location because of the comments of online bullies and trolls. Even though she was forced to move, Ms. Frazier has not cowered to the bullies and trolls; this young hero has had an aggressive response to the online bigoted cowards.

Do you recall what I said earlier in the book about comedian Richard Pryor saying that a black cop had to treat a black person worse than a white cop so the black cop could show that he was actually one of them (just like a white cop)? Well, has anyone noticed that two of the four cops involved in the murder of George Floyd were not white? One is black and the other is Asian (Laotian)—a recent arrival. I will let the reader make the connection between Richard Pryor's comment and the behavior of the non-white officers.

Allow me to repeat my Robert Kennedy quote: "Few men are willing to brave the disapproval of their fellows, the censure of their colleagues, the wrath of their society. Moral courage is a scarcer commodity than bravery in battle or great intelligence. Yet it is the one essential, vital quality of those who seek to change a world which yields most painfully to change." Ponder this quote in the context of the three aiding and abetting officers: Tou Thao, Thomas Lane, and J. Alexander Kueng—officers who failed to halt a fatal injustice.

I print the name of all four officers who were involved in this callous public murder. I print their names because they deserve credit for their deeds. The "justice" system may not indict them, but I do. If the "justice" system finds legal system loopholes to let these officers go free, then there is something really, really, wrong with the "justice" system. Where there is no justice, there *should be* no peace.

For her enlightenment, my writing advisor asked me to articulate the difference between my civil rights experiences in the 60s and the movement that has gone global since the killing of our brother, George Floyd. I was buoyed by her sincere interest in and her valuing what I am attempting to convey in this book. I responded by saying that her asking me to expound on these two civil rights matters that span a period of over 55 years made me seem like a sage—the term *sage* dates me, but that's not a bad thing. I have not only been an eyewitness and participant in civil rights history, but I have been dismayed by the progress or the lack thereof, during this span of time.

This is what I said to my writing advisor:

I am honored that you are interested in learning *my* perspective regarding the social justice movement of the 60s and since. The most noticeable differences that stand out this time—post George Floyd's death—is that this current social justice *movement* (I pray that it is not just a *moment*) involves many more white *people*, many more people of other races, and other peoples around the world. In the 60s, the thrust of the movement was desegregation/integration of public accommodations and along with that, a demand for better jobs and better housing.

During today's sea change (or tidal wave) for social justice, the demands—growing out of the heinous murder of George Floyd, captured on video—are for wholesale *systemic change* in the way that America treats and mistreats blacks physically, socially, emotionally, and economically. It seems that the video-captured murder of George Floyd woke up America to the point where America was willing to *hear* the long-standing petitions and grievances of black people. I do believe in God and I think that what is happening now is a providential move. I think that God has orchestrated the confluence of events to make this tidal wave of support for social justice so dynamic and widespread. This *seems* like an age of enlightenment in which white people are coming to realize what black people have been claiming all along—and white people seem more willing to deal with our truth.

In the 60s, we had President Lyndon Johnson—a Southerner—to be a champion for civil rights and voting rights. During these times, we have Donald Trump—a Northerner—to act as the antagonist against social justice; however, what is occurring today truly seems like a *mass* movement (as Dr. King would call it) of the people that seem determined to "let nobody turn us around" (as we sang in the 60s during our marches and demonstrations).

Now, in regards to the slogan, "Black Lives Matter," the racist and at best, the uninformed and uneducated, counter with "White Lives Matter" or "All Lives Matter." The latter two slogans are *understood*. "White Lives Matter" is a no-brainer—we all know that; that statement is manifested in all facets of American life; "All Lives Matter," even though it is meant to be a counter to "Black Lives Matter," is highly questionable. If all lives mattered and there was evidence of that, we wouldn't be talking about black lives matter.

When I first heard the slogan, "Black Lives Matter," I thought that the slogan should have more appropriately been named, "Black Lives Matter, Too." Being an amateur wordsmith, I thought that the latter slogan would convey more fully the meaning of the "Black Lives Matter" slogan. On further reflection, I think that the slogan "Black Lives Matter" is a *bold* statement that needed to be articulated just as it is. Adding "too" to the slogan would have softened the statement, I think. "Black Lives Matter" is a more "in your face" type statement, with a certain militancy about it. It is as if we are not *asking* others to buy into the assertion, it is more of a *demand* that whites *recognize* the validity of our claim and *act* accordingly.

After having said all that about Black Lives Matter, the above are my thoughts and may not represent the views and opinions of the Black Lives Matter organization. I am not a member of the organization, but I do plan to further research the organization and join very soon.

Prior to the brutal murder of George Floyd by Derek Chauvin and his three cohorts, I had come to the informed opinion that police unions defend accused police officers no matter what. The blatancy and the criminality of the acts that are so glaring are defended aggressively by police unions. It is euphemistic to call them unions; they act more like legal advocates for the crime family—a consigliere of sorts. Credibility is lost when *everything* becomes defensible.

Did you notice how cavalierly and callously that murderer Derek Chauvin kneeled on Mr. Floyd's neck? At least eight minutes and 46 seconds, why did he kneel so long? Did he think that this black man, biologically, had a greater tolerance for pain than white people do? Chauvin's disposition showed that what he was doing was no big deal; it was just a routine action carried out "in the line of duty." He looked so comfortable with his kill, probably thinking that the police union would have his back and that he would get to go home to his family.

It was as if Chauvin was snuffing out the life of an animal—a slow kill. One morning several years ago, I was looking out my office window and I saw a hawk in my parking lot; the hawk was just standing there—still—and I wondered why the hawk was just standing out in the open in the parking lot.

Observing more closely, I could see that the hawk was standing on the neck of a small animal—snuffing the life out of the animal until the animal couldn't breathe. When I discovered what was happening, I dashed out the door to run the hawk away and off his prey; however, the hawk grasped his prey in his claws and flew to a location further away and landed and resumed his killing position. The humanity in me created a reflex such that I wanted to save this animal's life—an *animal* that I did not even know.

I think that the *slow kill*, caught on video with sound, awakened the humanity in all people with a conscious and who value human life. In response to this inhuman act, people of all races, not just in Minneapolis and the United States, but all across the globe, rose up to decry police brutality. It was a beautiful sight to behold.

The sight of so many of us uniting for a just cause brought to mind the lyrics of the song, "We Are the World" (written in 1985 by Michael Jackson and Lionel Richie and produced by Quincy Jones and Michael Omartian). I will paraphrase the first stanza so as not to infringe on the work of others. The first stanza basically says that we, the world, must unite to answer the call of our time because people are dying. This song was written 35 years ago; I am hopeful that this song proves prophetic, and I am cautiously optimistic that at this point in time, we are answering the call.

The Confederate Flag and the Confederate Statues

Changing topics but not tone, here is what one writer had to say in defense of the Confederate flag:

> If you think the original meaning of this ever had anything to
> do with racism, you are in desperate need of a true education."

"Plenty of free black men, willingly fighting for the country they believed in, carried this flag into battle and were shot and killed by Lincoln's white soldiers. This flag has just as much white blood on it as it does black blood. It symbolized a kind of freedom we, white and black, have never tasted. It symbolized a country, not a race. In the information age, ignorance is a choice."

Yeah, ignorance is a choice and so are denial and racism. I wonder—but not really—why the Ku Klux Klan fly the Confederate flag? This Good Ole Boy, wanna be intellectual and historian, wants us to fall for the banana in the tail pipe gag. The explanation that Good Ole Boy wrote isn't worth a warm bucket of spit.

William T. Thompson, April 23, 1863, creator of the Confederate flag said this about the flag:

As a people we are fighting to maintain the Heaven-ordained supremacy of the white man over the inferior or colored race" and "as a national emblem, it is significant of our higher cause, the cause of the superior race. A white flag would thus be emblematical of our cause. Upon a red field would stand fourth our southern cross. Gemmed, preserving in beautiful contrast the red white and blue."

The confederate statutes go hand in hand with the Confederate flag; they represent the same things—hate and white supremacy! Hate for people who are not white and especially for black people. There is really no legitimate argument for defending either as public displays in the *United* States. *Personal, private* displays of the Confederate flag and confederate statutes can be argued. Such displays just tell us who you *really* are and that you want to "make America great again."

Government sanctioned public displays of these representations of hatred, slavery, white supremacy, and treason should not be allowed. If they are allowed, then those high ideals that this country loves to boast about and get choked up about are merely lofty words. I remember one night, as I was about to walk into the stadium at one of my son's football games out in some white enclave in rural America, I heard the announcer say, "Will you please rise, remove your hats, *and* place your hands over your hearts to honor the greatest country in the world." It was a given—it was baked in; he had nary a thought about the veracity of his claim and in that enclave, and I am sure that he knew that *all* who were gathered would agree.

Let me wax philosophical for a moment. When people live in an echo chamber, they have no pressure to conduct critical thinking regarding their views or their truth because everyone is saying the same thing—so it must be true. Limited exposure to *others* and the views and culture of *others* creates a very limited worldview.

I thought it apropos to mention here Plato's *The Republic* and his allegory of the cave. People in the cave had been chained since birth and could look neither to the left nor to the right. A fire was behind them and all that they could see were *shadows* on the cave wall in front of them of people, animals, and objects as they passed by. They truly believed that the shadows were the real thing.

One day one of the captives escaped and went out into the real world and eventually realized that what he and his fellow cave dwellers were experiencing were only shadows of the real things. When he came back into the cave, the escapee tried to educate the captives about the truth, but they would not here it. The truth was extremely difficult to swallow, so they killed the messenger and resumed rather comfortably their life of shadows.

One of my sons was enrolled in Gilmour Academy, a very private school, in Gates Mills, Ohio. Before we enrolled our son in the second grade, we inquired of the admissions representative regarding the racial make-up of the school. The number that she gave us indicated that minorities were well-represented; however, we belatedly discovered that the black minority was not well-represented.

I will cite two incidents to convey a feeling. One of the incidents occurred when my son brought home an image of the Union Jack flag to color; we took it to be the Confederate flag. The Union Jack is very similar to if not the same as the Confederate flag. We were so outraged that Gilmour Academy, such a prestigious school, would send an image of this flag home for our son to color that we made an appointment to meet with school officials. To school officials, the flag was the Union Jack, they say. To us, the flag was the Confederate flag.

I had commented to my wife on more than one occasion that the parents seemed like cookie-cutter parents: They were all white, drove SUVs, appeared to be soccer moms, had a superior disposition, and had minimal contact with black people or black culture or black concerns; the same may be said for the school officials. This elite school is really grooming leaders for the future, really. But their worldview is limited by their cave-like experience and they fail to see the Confederate flag in the Union Jack.

Another incident occurred with my son at Gilmour. He went on a bus field trip and he shared that some of the students didn't want to sit by him. We gave him the usual parent pep talk. We told him don't spend time worrying about it, just study hard and do his homework. His response to us was, "I gotta have friends." Those four words were so profound that we were speechless. I wondered—not really—from whom did these kids learn their exhibited behavior? In short order, we withdrew him from Gilmour Academy and enrolled him in a more diverse private school where he would not be made to feel like an outsider and where his concerns and ours were considered in every aspect of school life.

In 1966 and through 1970, Alabama white students didn't want to and didn't sit by me in class. In 2002, Ohio white students didn't want to and didn't sit by my son on the school bus. Thirty-two years and a different geography and a different economic demographic seem not to have made a difference. Shame.

CHAPTER 18

The Recapitulation

As I close this memoir, I am certain that I have left out some information that if I had thought of, I would have included. But I think that the narrative that I have presented is sufficient to convey my experiences, disappointments, hurts, and my experiential learning and the keenness of my observations and the depths of my thought about these observations. Any additional information would only be adding length—not breadth—to my narrative.

My hope is that the reader, after having read the book in its entirety, has gained a new perspective regarding those early days. Having read this memoir, I expect that the reader will appreciate not only the black perspective, but the recounting of facts by not only an *eyewitness to* the events, but a *participant in* the events.

As a starter, or as a tone setter, I presented historical information regarding who, exactly, is white. In that presentation, I provided the genesis of acceptance (or rejection) of one's whiteness. A discussion of the privileges attendant to being white was offered for the reader's consideration.

I provided some biographical information about myself. I expressed my thoughts concerning my entry into the world, where I—along with other black babies—was born in the *basement* of a segregated hospital. I attempted to portray what that birth circumstance portended for the remainder of the lives of the black children born in the circumstance. My family background and my early years were disclosed so that the reader could capture a *feel* for what life was like for me growing up.

In describing the most formative years of my life, I labored to give the reader a vivid sense of what it was like for me—and other black children—growing up and coming of age in the 50s and 60s in an almost totally segregated Alabama. In doing so, I wrote about being poor, attending overcrowded segregated schools, and participating in marches and sit-ins.

Prior to writing about my University of Alabama experiences, I laid down the most recent major, legal wranglings regarding the "separate but equal" doctrine and the desegregation prize. This was done so that my story regarding my university experiences could be contextualized. Along with that, I cited the struggles related to the first attempts of blacks to enroll at the University of Alabama.

All of the above were deliberately crafted as a springboard for jumping into those University of Alabama days. I described my first interaction with a University of Alabama official—the registrar, my white roommate, the social atmosphere, and the isolation.

I tried to paint a picture of the students' reaction to blacks and my professors' classroom demeanor. Of particular note were the derogatory comments of my Business Law professor and the reaction of white cafeteria diners to our black student presence. I paused for a moment to discuss various *recent* incidents and encounters with white folks that were reminiscent of the early days in Alabama.

I shared the confluence of events that led to my friends and I deciding to walk-on to play football for the Crimson Tide; nothing was planned—no forethought—regarding playing football for *our* university. In addition, I shared the reaction to our presence from the other players, the coaches, and the media. I also related attempts by officials to make us seem non-threatening and acceptable.

In closing out my football experiences, I discussed the matter of the academic scholarship and the *decisive* meeting with Assistant Head Football Coach Sam Bailey. My mixed emotions regarding the subject matter of the meeting were laid out. Coming to the realization that my football pilgrimage was at its end, I shared my thoughts and discussed my feelings of disappointment and relief.

I transitioned from my football experiences to conversations regarding what people were saying and writing about The First Five and my commentary on those opinions. I spent an inordinate amount of time discussing an article in *The St. Petersburg Times*. The article was very important in that it served as a prime example of (1) how even some well-meaning whites will defend the status quo, (2) how some whites want to place negative occurrences in the best light, and (3) how some whites diminish the value of the victimized.

Following my comments regarding *The St. Petersburg Times* article, I talked about certain people questioning the legitimacy of The First Five as *football players*. The argument was that we did not play in a recognized game— as though we had control over that. I answered those critics by using the subsequent comments of Coach Bear Bryant, the recognition by the University of Alabama History Department's Friends of History, and recognition by the University of Alabama A Club.

At length, I shared my feelings and presented evidence regarding the relative slow pace at which Coach Bryant was moving to integrate his lily white football squad; this was a sore spot with many Alabama fans who were convinced that Coach Bryant went as fast as he could toward integrating his team. I countered that notion with excerpts from Coach Bryant's sworn 1970 deposition.

After "ruffling feathers" with my comments about Coach Bryant's integration attempts, I talked about how my thoughts about those days were re-awakened and started me on this journey to set the record straight. Until I viewed portions of the HBO documentary *Breaking the Huddle*, I didn't think anyone remembered The First Five. A series of subsequent events were causative in the writing of this book.

Near the end of the book, I noted the changing of the guard—racially. I cited the 2019 racial makeup of the Crimson Tide football team and the proliferation of black players. I questioned—rhetorically—from where had all these black, academically qualified blacks come? I wrote that they were almost nonexistent when Tide coaches were *trying to recruit* them in the 60s.

I end the book with my interview with former Coach Pat Dye, which led into the case I made for affirmative action. Coach Dye took the football interview into an unexpected direction. I recorded that he was passionate about letting the world know that this country was built on the backs of black people. He spoke as someone who *needed* to get that fire out of his bones.

In terms of affirmative action, I commented that it is what is needed to level the playing field if black people are to ever get even. I make the point that to deny affirmative action as practice and policy, is to deny the advantages that whites enjoy by rigging the system at every turn to their advantage.

I have written about my First Five desegregation experiences in detail, while sharing my thoughts that are not only tangential to the Crimson Tide experience, but inseparable from the concoction of race that is practiced in this country. In addition to identifying events, situations, and incidents, I have worked to show the absurdity, silliness, and foolishness of some of these events, situations, and incidents.

I have experienced quite a lot in my 72 years living in this country as a black man. Oftentimes, our stories and experiences are written by and viewed through the lens of whites. This is one of the reasons that I chose to share from the perspective of a black man so that at the least, society would receive a balancing view as to what society has heard and processed through the eyes and perspective of white America.

My hope is that the white reader has kept an open mind regarding what I have shared. I have been brutal with my verbiage at times, partly due to the anger that has been built up in me and partly due to the situations and conditions demanding that I be brutal. I pulled no punches, I have shared what *I know* that America needs to hear. I do not apologize for *my* truth; moreover, I believe that my truth should receive apologies.

This is what I had written prior to the callous murder of George Floyd and the ongoing aftermath: My wish for America going forward is that race *per se*, will become a null and void issue in our dealings with each other as human beings and as equals. The direction in which America is heading now is in reverse. With Donald John Trump at the helm and his Republican puppeteers in lock step with him, I envision that America will slip further into the abyss of racism, hate, and injustice.

Since writing the above statement pre-George Floyd's murder, I feel very encouraged in the aftermath of his murder. I am elated that we have many others from many different races who have indicated that they understand our plight and are willing to help in addressing our grievances. Even large corporations joined the cause. These things coupled with the ouster of Donald Trump her, we can begin to close the divide. Glory be to God.

I feel so much better that I have been able to complete this memoir. It has allowed me to empty myself of many of my frustrations and indignation with racial injustice and its continuation for the foreseeable future. My strategy in presenting my case in this memoir is one of "tough love." History shows us that sugar coating the truth has not worked. We need to own up to our racist past (and present) and take corrective action with all deliberate speed. Dick Gregory once opined that America will be destroyed from within long before it will be destroyed from without.

APPENDIX A

Excerpts from the 1970 Deposition

IN THE DISTRICT COURT OF THE UNITED STATES FOR THE
NORTHERN DISTRICT OF ALABAMA, WESTERN DIVISION
AFRO-AMERICAN ASSOCIATION OF THE UNIVERSITY OF
ALABAMA, et al,

Plaintiffs,	)	
Vs.	)	No. 69-422-W
PAUL "BEAR" BRYANT, Athletic	)	
Director and Head Football	)	
Coach of the University of	)	
Ala, et al,		
Defendants,	)	

Tuscaloosa, Alabama
July 8, 1970

BEFORE:
CARMEN ZEGARELLI, Comissioner

APPEARANCES:
Mr. U. W. CLEMON of the firm Adams, Baker & Clemon, Masonic Temple
Building, Birmingham, Alabama; and MR. A. J. COOER, JR., of the firm
Crawford, Fields & Cooper, Mobile, Alabama, appearing on behalf of the
Plaintiff.

MESSRS. ANDREW J. THOMAS an WILLIAM C. KNIGHT, JR., of the
firm Thomas, Toliaferro, Forman, Burr and Murray, Bank for Savings
Building, Birmingham, Alabama, and MR. J. RUFUS BEALLE, University
of Alabama, and MR. GEORGE T. DRIVER, University of Alabama,
appearing on behalf of the Defendants.

Q. Coach Bryant, in the answers to interrogatories, to your interrogatories, you indicated, I believe that there were certain black athletes that had been offered scholarships for the 1969 football season, and you indicated that all of those athletes either went elsewhere or did not qualify academically. Mr. Thomas, do you have a copy of it? It is Exhibit I in the interrogatories which you sent to us on the 1ˢᵗ of July?

A   That would be year before last; there were three in particular.

Q   Excuse me, go ahead.

Q   Let me just talk about them as you list them and ask you about each one of them. Now, with reference to Bert Cooper?

A   Oh, that is really for 1970; that was for this coming year.

Q   O.K. All right.
     Now, did Bert Cooper indicate to you that he was going to attend another school as opposed to the University?

A   Unfortunately he did. ...I visited with the boy and his mother and father over the phone a time or two, but we would like very much to have had him, I will tell you that, but I found out since then, well, I didn't learn until today, telling me in there he only made about a ten or eleven on the ACT. We didn't know that then; we were recommending him for scholarship, wanted him very much.

Q   Now, with reference to Virgil Pearson, Fairfield, Alabama, did he fail to qualify academically?

A   We were talking about him with my staff, I really don't remember him, but we did not recommend him for scholarship.

Q   All right.
     Isaac Jackson, Coach Bryant, Macon, Georgia?

A   Well, Isaac Jackson we couldn't get very interested in us up here and we think he is a terrific football player and still would like to have him. It is not settled yet where he is going, but based on his academic standing, we didn't think he could get in there, and we tried to get him to visit, never could even get him to visit.

Q   Do you know whether Mr. Jackson scored less than 17 on the ACT?

A   I don't know what he did; ...

Q   All right.

Now, Jerry Moses, Waterloo, Iowa?

A   Jerry Moses is probably, based on my people that sought him, and I think saw one game, I may be wrong on that, probably the best prospect running back in America,... And one time he was coming for a visit with us, and there was some mix-up; when he got to the airport...the family thought we were inviting them, and that is a violation of the rules to do that, and we couldn't do that. ...And then he told us he wasn't interested and we never could get him back...In fact, I sent back out there and said he was going to Notre Dame.

Q   Al right. Now, Mr. James Ricky Brown of Montgomery, St. Jude Hospital, has he been accepted at the University of Alabama?

A   I don't know, sir.

Q   Did you recruit him?

A   The name doesn't hit me.

Q   O.K.

A   We didn't offer to recommend a scholarship.

Q   Do you know whether he scored less than 17 on the ACT?

A   I don't know; our people in there may know.

Q   Mr. John King of Harvest, Alabama?

A   Name means nothing to me; I don't know.

Q   In other words, you didn't request—didn't recruit him yourself?

A   He may have been on our list, but we did not offer him a scholarship...

Q   Mr. James Bonds of Russelville?

A   We thought he was a prospect and he was an academic casualty as far as we were concerned.

Q   Did he score less than 17 on the ACT?

A   I don't know what he scored, but when we had to make a decision, we wanted him, we thought he was a prospect.

Q   All right. Ralph McGill of Miami, Oklahoma?

A   Well, there is one that I thought we had, really. Ralph is from down in Florida, and, of course, you know they won the National Championship, Junior College, that made All-American. We had our coaches watching him, following him, and he is a terrific prospect... Ralph sat in my office in there and told me that he thought, first place, he knew he could make the team; of course, he can make anybody's team, I think; and he said he thought this was what he wanted to do and we talked, I told him; I said, now, Ralph, I don't know, we never had a black football player on our squad and might be problems; we have them with white ones, probably have them with anybody. I said, if that is true, all I want to know is, you come to me. So, we had one of the Home-Coming Queens that took him out, and when he went back, I thought we were going to get him, and then he cooled off and said he wasn't coming, and I don't know what happened; I thought maybe something had happened while he was here. I just don't know...Anyway, we lost him to Tulsa.

Q   All right. Isiah Harris of Edmondson, Arkansas?

A   ...We were very impressed with him...we pulled off on him because of his grades and ACT.

Q   There is another one by the name of David Chambliss?

A   That is not the one; we need your help to get this one in school; he made a 13, I believe, on ACT, and he is going to take it again.

Q   Do you recall, coach, whether Don Howard and David Chambliss failed to qualify academically for scholarship?

A   I don't know, but we didn't think they qualified athletically.

All right, I will put it this way. I didn't have them on my list; if they played on the same team, I am sure we saw them.

Q   Do you recall Johnny Corbit of Valdosta, Georgia?

A   No. I went down to Valdosta to try to recruit a couple of kids and he wasn't one of them, quarterback and linebacker.

Q   Do you know whether he was offered a scholarship?

A   He was not here.

Q   Do you recall whether you talked with him?

A   I am sure my scout and his coach are very close to Pat Dye, who scouts that area, and the two boys we were after in Valdosta, we lost them both to the University of Georgia; they had a real fine football team; they played for the Championship.

Q   How about Curtis Gray from Moundville, Alabama?

A   He can fly and he doesn't qualify academically, but we are hoping that he will go to Junior College since we recommended him to the same place where McGill went and will come back here.

Q   All right.

A   He will have to work and get his grades up, but we think he is a prospect.

Q   Do you recall Lepald Sterling of Pahokee, Florida, Coach C. W. Pell?

A   I don't recall him, but I believe there is one of the kids at – one that Clem and I were talking about, one of our coaches saw him, may not be, so I had better not say that, but thought he was an athlete, but there we had the academic thing.

Q   Which of your coaches had contact with him, do you know?

A   Ralph Jenito had been working Florida and then this year Hayden Riley did most of it.

Q   Now, Coach, do you remember Arthur Battle of Lee High School in Huntsville who was a back?

A   I remember him, and we did not go after him.

Q   All right.

Q   ...can you think of any of the names of any black athletes, any other ones other than those listed on your answers to interrogatories who were checked by your staff for the fall football season of 1969?

A   Well, we probably checked fifty, sixty, seventy schools; but in answer to your specific question, I can tell you some good ones like Bo Mathews at Huntsville. We signed him and he do not even graduate from high school.

Q   Bo Mathews in Huntsville?

A   Yes; he is a terrific athlete.

Q   Do you know what high school he went to?

A   He went to one where Mr. Crews is superintendent; I forget which one is which; we recommended him; we were hoping that he will go to Miami, Oklahoma, and we will set him back. If it would have been close on his ACT, we were going to ask him to take it again and try any way in the world to get him in, because he is a terrific football player, but I think he made something like 8 or 9 on his ACT; I can recall we had a kid at Cleveland, talking about good ones, that we worked real hard on year before last and we lost him to all people, to Chattanooga, not that Chattanooga is not a good school.

Q   Do you know the boy's name?

A   Walker or Waller, I had him in my home; I remember that, and a real great one. Boy from Tupelo, Mississippi, named Dowsing, Old Mississippi State right now will probably beat our tail and we thought we had him.

Q   Would that be Frank Dowsey?

A   Yes, we lost him to Mississippi and same year the Owens kid up here at Fairfield; I had him in my home and dressing room at the — after the L.S. U. game and he looked me in the teeth and said he wanted to come to Alabama and wanted to be here, but we lost him to Auburn.

Q   Now, with respect to James Owens, Coach Bryant, isn't it true that you didn't approach him until after Auburn had signed him?

A   Owens? We worked on him the entire year. I had him in my home during the season, had him down to the game, had him over to the dorm.

Q   Did you offer him a scholarship?

A   Yeah; and shook hands on it and he accepted it verbally; me personally.

Q   That is also true of Frank Dowsey?

A   Oh, yes; we thought we had Frank and this kid both and, of course, Owens is a good prospect, good football player, and he didn't qualify for scholarship at Auburn until this summer. Had him on some kind of deal, but this Dowsey is a real fine student, and I think his mother is an English Teacher and he just ran about a 9-6 or 9-7 over at Mississippi State; he was a good one, real good one.

Q   Do you recall Greg E. Davis, I think he was from Tennessee.

A   I believe that is the kid from Cleveland; from Cleveland, Tennessee.

Q   Correct.

A   Yeah, we offered him a scholarship.

Q   Do you recall the black athletes, Jim Salis, Larry Horton and Jeff Bailey who were students, I take it, at Elsworth Junior College in Centerville, Iowa?

A   Well, we got one kid from up there; we went out there, but I shouldn't know if they expressed an interest, and we didn't – no, I don't recall whether it was black or white; I don't know.

Q   Do you recall whether they were offered scholarships?

A   Well, if they were actually offered one, I would have to approve it; the way we have it set up now, two or three years I let somebody else do it, but I do it myself; I would have to get Rogers in there, he was the one that went out there before I would know what I told him.

Q   All right.

Do you recall the black athletes Clarence Threatt, Sylvester McKinney and Albert Young of East Highland High School in Sylacauga?

A   No.

Q   Do you recall whether you made them an offer?

A   I know we did not make them an offer; we didn't think they qualified athletically.

Q   All right, sir. Now, also in your answers to interrogatories, you indicate that there are certain black high school Juniors who are athletes, and presumably you have been looking at them and you say you have not made any contact with them; is that correct?

A   Well, this Cleveland kid down here at Centerville, we certainly made no contact with him; he was in to see me the other day, and two or three weeks ago.

Q   Is that the one at Bibb County High School?

A   Right; we have already, I have told him that personal we wanted him and we do want him he can play any one of three sports, and we want him very much and we have told him we recommended him for Scholarship and got the Alumnae working on him down there; I am scared to death that he will sign a baseball contract; he had a terrific year in baseball.

Q   That would be Charles Cleveland?

A   Right.

Q   What score did he make on the ACT?

A   Don't know yet; he was coming to take it – was going to take it this summer – don't know whether he has taken it now or is going to take it the next time, but when he was in here – but in answer to your question, I don't know, we are going to offer him – or we want him, let's put it this way.

Q   Now, these –

A   I will tell you another one we want very much, if you have any influence. I am – a kid in Miami, Oklahoma, from North Carolina, he is another Mike Garrett.

Q   Would that be Ken Garrett?

A   Yes, and he is a good one.

Q   I see you list Ken Garrett in the answers to your – to our interrogatories, but you do not list Charles Cleveland.

Can you think of the names of any other juniors in High School who are black and on whom you have been–

A   Already working on?

Q   Yes.

A   Paul Caruthers, Lafayette, Georgia; Larry Matkins; Burlington, North Carolina; Calvin Gulley, Blount High School, Mobile, Alabama; James Hammond, Sparkman High School, for practical purposes, it would be Huntsville, Alabama.. We missed a boy up there, big old fine looking boy; kind of borderline. After they went in and signed him, we wished we had; lost him to Georgia. Conreich Holloway, Lee High School, Huntsville, Alabama; Marshall Mills, Morristown, Tennessee; Louis Walker, Enterprise, Alabama; John Freeman, Oakman, Alabama; Daniel Buggs, Avondale High School, Atlanta, Georgia; Ken Garrett, Northeast Junior College, Miami, Oklahoma.

Q   Those are the only ones you know of?

A   They –

Q   In addition to those you mentioned? Let me ask you this. Are you still working with Jeff Cherner in Pritchard? MR. GRYSKA: He is what we call, I don't know what term you have been using, we are looking at him.

A   He is suspect; we are going to watch him.

Q   How about Sylvester Croom, Tuscaloosa?

A   He is suspect.

Q   And Jimmy Lewis, Jackson, Mississippi?

A   A Quarterback; we will classify him a prospect.

Q   Calvin Callaway of Pritchard, Alabama?

A   He is suspect.

Q O. K.

A I hope the hell this list doesn't get to our opponents.

Q Well, I most certainly am not going to release any information.

Q ...Andrew Pernell went out for the team in 1967, did he not?

A I think Andrew came out the spring after Doc, but anyway, he did; Andrew was out there and Andrew stayed, I think, longer than any of them, but the two that we have had out there that might have helped us someday were, doing good, were Doc and Andrew.

Q All right. Now, Andrew Pernell was on some type of community scholarship, was he not?

A We didn't know that, of course; he had been out there, I guess, a year before that came up. He didn't put it on his first – when he filled out our first eligibility blank and it turned out he was getting some kind of loan or help in some way from a church, I believe that is right, Presbyterian or something.

Well, anyway, when that came about we had – there was five of them, four white boys and Andrew and have a rule, a Conference rule that prohibits them from playing unless they were counted in our scholarship number, and of course, they were not; and even if we would have wanted to have counted them, we couldn't have, because we were out.

I didn't like – I was in sympathy, particularly with Andrew and a boy named Orville, Orville worked and paid a terrific price to be out there. Anyway, we called the Commissioner, and then later we had correspondence back and forth, we had to ask them to not come out, and there was five of them, and Pernell was one of them.

Q Was Pernell the only black?

A Of the group; yes, sir.

Q And the only reason, as far as you know, why Andrew Pernell was asked not to come back was because he was receiving this scholarship paid?

A As far as I know. We were already practicing, happened on the 6th of September, we had been practicing a week and were violating the rule by having him out there, but didn't know it.

Q Did you offer Pernell a scholarship or grant-in-aid for the following year?

A   No.

Q   Offer any of the white fellows one?

A   No.

Q   All right.

A   We can carry over. If it was now, I would not, because I can carry it over until next year, but two of them, Orville and Pernell, If – see, we already started and if we had any left, we couldn't use them anyway; I don't know; I would have offered him one then, because they worked and been out there, and, heck, if they wasn't going to play, and might have played some day, but wasn't going to play, I would have offered those two one. You can contribute to winning without playing, because someone has to be the other team, but didn't have one at that time.

Q   Do you recall the names of the others members of the group who were told that they have to –

A   Well, Clem might, but the two that I was most concerned with was Orville, Jim Orville.

Q   Jim Orville?

A   And Andrew Pernell was the two that I was really in sympathy with.

Q   …Now, coach, you did say that Andrew Pernell had to play for a year before you discovered he was on a community scholarship?

A   I think he was out there for an entire year – I know he was out there for a year, because I remember he played a little in the spring game or scrimmage or something we had over there.

Q   Might have been as much as a year and a half?

A   Possibly; possibly, but on the eligibility blank, we have them all filled out and the first year he didn't have that down, he was getting – I believe it was a loan, I am not sure, and then the second year it was brought to my attention: I don't know how; much have been from eligibility blank again, but we had been practicing about a week before we even knew it, and actually we were in violation of the rules and didn't know it.

Q   …All right. Now, can you think of any instance in which any of your recruiters, that is staff recruiters, visited any all black high school prior to January, 1968?

A   Clem, have we? Didn't Jack have a clinic for them? When was that?
MR. GRYSKA: I don't know.

A   I really don't know.

Q   I guess that the answer to that question would be no?

A   I said I don't know, I can't answer that.
MR. GRYSKA: It would be this way. Again, Coach Bryant, you mentioned the gentleman that Ellis Taylor called you about from Jasper, if we had a specific phone call or letter about an outstanding athlete, we would go.

A   The coach talked with me down at the Clinic and I sent up there and had the boy checked and our people didn't think he could play.

Q   When was that?

A   I believe it was about '67; it would have been before your questionnaire.

Q   Would you have any record which would reflect that?

A   No; probably wouldn't; it would be three or four years ago; probably came back and told me they didn't think he could play.

Q   …In your tenure as being one of the top college football coaches, would you say that you have gotten to know and become friends with most of the other top football coaches in the nation?

A   I know most of them. I don't know — I am not the most popular guy in the world, not at home or here or anywhere; but I certainly know most of them; yes.

Q   Have you ever, or has anyone of your staff members, as you know, attempted to discuss with these other coaches and their staff, means whereby you could increase the number or means by which you could recruit black ball players?

A   No, I haven't been interested in that or felt it necessary; I have in the last year, because John McKay, of course, has had a lot of black ball plyers and they have just arrived here; you know, but I have talked with him about it.

Q   Given the success that other colleges have had in recruiting black ball players from Alabama, could you tell us why you think the University of Alabama hasn't been able to obtain black ball players?

A   Well, first of all, I don't think that business about success of other people, I don't know, there haven't been many, to begin with, and secondly, as I say, up until about two or three years ago, we rarely ever heard of one. And since then, the ones that we have tried to recruit, we have gone over individually on – and I wish we – wish I knew why we didn't get them, but – particularly Dowsey and Owens.

Q   All right. Could you tell me the benefits which accrue to a ball player, aside from the academic benefits and the personal physical benefits for graduating from the University of Alabama and having been a Varsity member of your team?

Q   ...Be a bit more specific, having been a Varsity member of one of your squads, would a person have a much better opportunity to go on to coaching or professional activities in the field of sports?

A   Well, I would certainly hope so, yes.

Q   Coach, has any alumni or administration or other type of pressure been applied to you adverse to your having black athletes on your team?

MR. THOMAS: I don't know that that question is relevant; I don't know what you are driving at and I object to that question and ask Coach not to answer it.

MR. COOPER: O.K., that is all.

MR. THOMAS: I have no questions.

FURTHER DEPONENT SAITH NOT

APPENDIX B

Bottom of Form

1963 FOOTBALL SCHEDULE

DATE	TEAM	PLACE
Sept. 21	Virginia Polytechnic Institute	Birmingham (N)
Sept. 28	Southern Mississippi	Mobile
Oct. 5	Mississippi	Jackson
Oct. 12	Vanderbilt	Tuscaloosa
Oct. 19	Tennessee	Knoxville
Oct. 26	Clemson	Tuscaloosa
Nov. 2	Mississippi State	Tuscaloosa (HC)
Nov. 9	Louisiana State University	Birmingham
Nov. 16	Miami	Miami (N)
Nov. 30	Auburn	Birmingham

This program comes to you with the compliments of the University of Alabama National Alumni Association and is distributed courtesy of CIRCLE K

ANNUAL SPRING

FOOTBALL GAME

REDS
VS.
WHITES

UNIVERSITY OF ALABAMA
KICKOFF 3:00 P.M.
DENNY STADIUM
MAY 4, 1968

WHITE SQUAD

No.	NAME	Pos.	Hgt.	Wgt.	Class	Hometown
10	David Beddingfield	QB	6-2	190	Junior	Hamilton
11	Neb Hayden	QB	6-0	184	Soph	Charlotte, N.C.
17	Oran Buck	K	6-0	200	Soph	Oak Ridge, Tenn.
19	Norris Hamer	DE	6-1	190	Senior	Tarrant
20	Niles Prestage	K	5-11	180	Junior	Huntsville
21	Red Stokley	FLK	5-11	160	Soph	Lapeer, Mich.
23	Gary Stephenson	FLK-DHB	5-7	165	Fresh	Oneonta
24	Danny Sikes	DHB	5-11	185	Soph	Memphis, Tenn.
26	Al Harvey	DHB	6-0	178	Fresh	Atlanta, Ga.
28	Mike Dean	DHB	6-2	170	Junior	Columbus, Ga.
29	Erwin Arnold	FLK-OE	5-11	172	Junior	Atlanta, Ga.
31	Ken Emerson	S	6-1	185	Soph	Columbus, Ga.
33	Eddie Bentley	DHB	5-11	180	Soph	Cullman
34	Tom Keywood	DHB	6-1	180	Soph	Dothan
35	Phil Chaffin	FB	5-10	175	Soph	Huntsville
36	Wayne Owen	R-LB	5-10	185	Senior	Gadsden
37	Andrew Pernell	FLK	5-8	160	Junior	Gadsden
38	Tommy Wade	TB-S	6-2	180	Junior	Dothan
42	Pete Moore	S	5-11	190	Junior	Bessemer
50	Danny Thomas	C	6-0	195	Soph	Hopkinsville, Ky.
51	Don Spruiell	C	6-2	210	Soph	Clinton, Tenn.
52	Mike Hand	LB	6-2	205	Soph	Sulligent
55	Mike Hall	C	5-11	195	Soph	Tuscumbia
56	Fred Marshall	LB	6-0	220	Senior	Hartselle
60	Sam Gellerstedt	MG	5-9	175	Soph	Tarrant
61	Ronnie Summerford	LB	5-8	185	Soph	Montgomery
63	Charles Ferguson	LB	5-7	190	Soph	Pelham, Ga.
64	Harvey Beaden	LB	5-10	175	Soph	Birmingham
65	Mike Reilly	OG	6-1	205	Soph	Bessemer
66	Tommy Israel	MG	6-1	194	Junior	Columbus, Ga.
68	Dale Rozncla	OT	6-2	198	Senior	Mobile
69	Alvin Samples	LB	6-2	215	Junior	Haleyville
70	Steve Doran	OG	6-1	225	Soph	Enterprise
71	Roger Rister	OT	6-2	190	Junior	Columbus Grove, Ohio
72	Gene England	OG	6-0	212	Junior	Glasgow, Ky.
73	Ken Wilder	OT	6-2	200	Senior	Columbus
74	Jay McCormick	DT	6-2	215	Junior	Columbus
75	George Boze	OT	6-2	225	Soph	Mississippi City, Miss.
76	Don Harris	OT	6-2	230	Junior	Nashville, Tenn.
77	Junior Davis	OT	6-2	214	Senior	Memphis, Tenn.
79	Jim Patterson	OG	6-3	209	Soph	Vincent
81	Jack McKewen	DE	6-1	215	Junior	Birmingham
82	Mike Ford	OE	6-1	210	Junior	Amandale, Va.
83	Hunter Husband	OE	6-5	215	Junior	Nashville, Tenn.
84	Jim Simmons	OE	6-4	210	Soph	Mountain Brook
85	Ken James	DE	6-3	200	Soph	Yazoo City, Miss.
86	Wayne Rhonds	DE	6-1½	180	Soph	Columbus, Ga.
87	Griff Langston	DE	6-0	178	Soph	Jackson, Miss
88	George Ranager	FLK-OE	5-11	175	Soph	Birmingham
89	Conrad Fowler	FLK-OE	6-3	199	Senior	Columbiana

INJURED AND UNABLE TO PLAY: Phander Perry Willis of Dadeville, mideyman Mike Sasser of Brewton, and Danny Payne of Anniston, tower Johnny Johnston of Birmingham, fullback Mickey Lee of Enterprise, midcyman Leslie Roberts of Haleyville, tailback Denny Johnson of Birmingham, guard Wayne Vardaman of Selma.

RED SQUAD

No.	NAME	Pos.	Hgt.	Wgt.	Class	Hometown
15	Scott Hunter	QB	6-2	202	Soph	Hamilton
16	Ronnie Richardson	QB	6-0	175	Fresh	Columbus, Ga.
17	Benny Rippetoe	QB	6-2	175	Soph	Greenville, Tenn.
21	Pete DeBello	FLK	5-9	170	Junior	Westwood, N.J.
23	Donnie Sutton	FLK-DHB	5-10	179	Senior	Enterprise
24	Tommy Weigand	TB-DHB	5-10	175	Fresh	Roger, Ga.
25	Jerry Cash	FLK-DHB	6-1	173	Soph	Birmingham
28	Larry Hehn	TB	5-10	175	Soph	Birmingham
30	Roger Crowson	FBR	6-4	210	Senior	Bessemer
32	Pete Jilleba	FB	6-2	188	Junior	Bessemer
33	Glenn Cole	R	5-11	180	Senior	Livingston
37	Danny Snakley	R	5-9	180	Soph	Geraldine
38	Woodie Husband	LB	6-0	205	Soph	Nashville, Tenn.
40	Buddy Seay	DHB	5-10	180	Soph	Dadeville
41	Robert Higginbotham	DHB	6-0	180	Senior	Bessemer
44	Vinnie Schilleci	DE	6-8	165	Senior	Birmingham
45	Ed Morgan	S	5-11	190	Soph	Bessemer
46	Bill Blair	S	6-0	170	Senior	Hattiesburg, Miss.
47	Richard Ferguson	OG	5-9	185	Soph	Nashville, Tenn.
48	Van Seary	OG	5-9	180	Fresh	Fort Payne
49	Mike Cox	K	5-11	160	Fresh	Jackson
50	Howard Stephens	C-LB	5-10	195	Soph	Town Creek
51	Ronnie Roddam	C-LB	6-0	198	Junior	Thomasville, Ga.
52	Richard Grammar	G	6-1	200	Junior	Hartselle
53	Pepo Koch	LB	6-2	205	Junior	Demopolis
54	Mike Houston	DT	6-2	230	Soph	Franklin, Ky.
56	Bob Childs	LB	6-1	198	Senior	Montgomery
60	Roger Womack	G	5-10	180	Senior	Tifton, Ga.
61	Bob Ferguson	G	5-11	195	Soph	Birmingham
62	Randy Brown	OT	6-1	213	Junior	Scottsville, N.Y.
63	Steve Clay	LB	6-2	195	Junior	Gadsden
64	Reid Drinkard	OG	6-1	197	Soph	Linden
65	Wayne McNutt	MG	5-11	190	Soph	Haleyville
66	Don Gossett	MG	6-0	190	Soph	Knoxville, Tenn.
67	Sid Roche	MG	5-11	185	Junior	Columbus, Ga.
68	Larry Campbell	OT	6-2	200	Junior	Blountsville
70	Paul Boschung	OT	6-3	240	Senior	Tuscaloosa
72	Randy Barron	OT-DT	6-5	228	Senior	Dadeville
73	Billy Strickland	DT	6-2	235	Soph	Birmingham
76	Jim Anvil	OT	6-2	220	Junior	Dothan
77	Morris Mousseu	OT	6-1	200	Soph	Columbus, Ga.
78	Neb Roberts	MG	5-6	180	Fresh	Moscow, Idaho
79	Danny Ford	OT	6-2	220	Junior	Gadsden
80	Bobby Swafford	OE	6-1	180	Junior	Gadsden
81	Clyde Butler	DE	6-2	220	Soph	Heflin
83	Ed Lindley	FLK	5-11	190	Soph	Scottsboro
84	Hal Wilcut	OE	5-11	175	Soph	Birmingham
85	Terry DuBose	DE	6-2	205	Soph	Tuscaloosa
86	Dennis Dixon	DE	6-2	195	Soph	Andalusia
87	Robert Deligan	DE	6-2	190	Soph	Jacksonville, Fla.
88	Lane Lawley	DE	6-2	200	Fresh	Hartshorne, Okla.
89	Bob Montgomery	DE	6-0	190	Soph	Shelbyville, Ky.

University of Alabama
Department of Athletics
University, Alabama 35486

The Crimson Tide

March 20, 1967

National Football Champions
1961, 1964, and 1965

Memorandum to: Dr. Frank A. Rose
                   Dr. Jeff Bennett

SUBJECT   :   COLORED ATHLETES

1. We have not actively attempted to recruit any
colored athletes in the State because we have had none that we felt
qualified both athletically and academically. We were interested in
one from Huntsville who was a good athlete, but did not qualify academically. There was another one from a local school in Northport who
were were interested in but he was expelled from school before graduating.

2. We are genuinely interested in two local athletes
from the Northport School who have another year in high school. We
are watching their progress both athletically and academically. I have
discussed the possibilities of these two youngsters with the high school
coach, and the father of one of them.

3. I guess we have had a few inquiries and copies of our
replies are available. We have had only one athlete to discuss the
possibility of being a candidate for the team. He came to see me this
past fall, and was told we would be glad to have him after taking his
physical examination, and filling out the eligibility blank as any other
prospective athlete. He did not report for practice. He visited me in
my office again around midterm and said that the reason he did not report
for practice in September was that he was in the school of Engineering
and thought he would be unable to adequately adapt himself to the academic
problems and practice football at the same time. We, of course, told
him that he would be treated like any other candidate. We also discussed
this candidate with our squad, making sure they understood that he was a
candidate like themselves,and would receive the same treatment from the

Rose Bowl
1926-1927
1931-1935-1938
1946

Sugar Bowl
1945-1948
1962-1964
1967

Orange Bowl
1943
1953
1963-1965-1966

Cotton Bowl
1942
1954

Bluebonnet Bowl
1960

Liberty Bowl
1959

166

-2-

staff and other members of the squad.

    4. At our Annual Coaching Clinic in August, we have from thirty to fifty colored coaches in attendance. This has been true for a number of years. Some of these coaches have attended our annual coaches banquet which is held in conjunction with our clinic.

    5. On numerous occasions we have colored coaches and players visit our practice, both in the spring and fall.

    6. Finally, we do not plan to recruit colored athletes from out-of-the-State at this time, but certainly would be interested in any who qualify within the State.

Respectfully,

Paul W. Bryant
Director of Athletics

UNIVERSITY OF ALABAMA
UNIVERSITY, ALABAMA 35486

OFFICE FOR ACADEMIC AFFAIRS   August 19, 1968

MEMORANDUM

TO: Dr. David Mathews

FROM: Willard F. Gray

     You may be interested to know that on Thursday, August 15, I met with Coach Bryant, Mr. Edward Nall, and Mr. Moses Jones to permit the students to discuss with Coach Bryant the complaints which they had registered in an earlier meeting which I attended.

     As you might readily imagine, Coach Bryant was on the offensive throughout the conversation, and the meeting resulted in a rather one-sided score. All in all, the discussion was a most cordial one and the students left with a pledge to assist with recruitment of outstanding, well-qualified, black athletes.

     If you should desire additional information on the meeting, I shall be pleased to discuss the matter with you.

W. F. G.

WFG/ll

NEWS

Gifts Sought for Scholarship Program

In early May, the Student Opportunity Scholarship office received a letter from one of its scholarship students, now a junior. Here is part of it:

"I received your letter informing me that I could not expect $2,070 from the Student Opportunity Scholarship program. However, I was quite honest in completing my application for renewal, since I do not have any other sources to rely on for educational funds except yours. My family's income is only about $3800 a year.

"When I was a freshman, I was among a group of five black athletes who were the first to try out for any sport here at the University of Alabama —and later I was the first black to make the varsity football squad. When I returned this past August for practice, after two years, the head coach informed me that I was ineligible to play because I was getting this Student Opportunity Scholarship. Consequently, I had a choice between playing football or receiving this scholarship. To me there was no choice since my education is dependent on your aid."

A phone call to Andy, the Student Opportunity scholar, gave us further information. Five black students had gone out for the varsity squad. None was offered financial aid by the university. Four dropped out, but Andy continued to practice. He was academically eligible for the team; he was a good athlete. But a varsity football player who was black could be regarded by some as an embarrassment to the University of Alabama. Whether this had anything to do with Andy's being told he could not be on the team because he had received a scholarship is a matter of speculation.

Andy's plight is not unique. Many black students face such difficulties. All their problems are magnified by the need for considerable financial assistance to stay in college.

Andy's plight is now the plight of the Student Opportunity Scholarship program. We have the help of a number of congregations, especially those which have surplus student aid funds, and of individuals who send designated gifts. This is especially helpful this year, when our allocation from the Fund for Freedom has been cut through circumstances beyond the scholarship program's control. Designated gifts may be sent to Student Opportunity Scholarships, 425 Witherspoon Building, Philadelphia, Pa. 19107, for this program in which the Board of Christian Education and the Board of National Missions cooperate.

—Wilmina M. Rowland

CREDITS: Cover, P. 7: Carl G. Karsch; Pp. 8, 9 (lower), 34: Official Photographer of New York State; P. 9 (top): Janet Harbison; Pp. 10, 11, 18, 19: drawings by Peter Petraglia; Pp. 14, 15: G. Arvid Peterson; P. 20: United Press International Ltd.; P. 38: drawing by Helen Stone.

Hanover College Receives $2.5 Million Bequest

The late J. Graham Brown spent only a year (1899-1900) at Hanover College in Indiana, yet he considered the United Presbyterian-related school his alma mater. After he had amassed a fortune through extensive timberland holdings, he contributed nearly $2 million to Hanover—with the stipulation that all his gifts be used for buildings. A campus center and a chapel are two of the structures built with the funds.

This past spring, the eighty-seven-year-old philanthropist died; in his will Hanover received a bequest of $2.5 million, the largest single gift to an institution. The bulk of Brown's $100-million estate went to the J. Graham Brown Foundation, which makes annual contributions to a number of charities and welfare agencies.

FOR THE RECORD

ANNIVERSARIES:

150th. First, Ashland, Ky. (the Rev. Heinrich B. Eiler, pastor).

125th. Gray Stone, Leechburg, Pa. (the Rev. H. D. Hough, pastor).

100th. First, Santa Barbara, Calif. (the Rev. Lawrence E. Fisher, pastor).

Red Oak, Iowa (the Rev. James E. Griffes, pastor).

Eliot, Lowell, Mass. (the Rev. Paul F. Ketchum, pastor).

Carmel, Lake Crystal, Minn. (the Rev. Walter E. Ulrich, pastor).

65th. Highland Park, Mich. (the Rev. Russell W. Durler, pastor).

60th. Llanerch, Havertown, Pa. (the Rev. John Franklin McCleary, pastor).

DEDICATIONS:

Westminster, Port Hueneme, Calif. (the Rev. Warren V. Porter, pastor), of a new sanctuary.

Florida Presbyterian College, St. Petersburg, Fla. (Dr. Billy O. Wireman, president), of the new Bininger Center for the Performing Arts, named in honor of the Reverend and Mrs. Clem Edward Bininger, pastor of the First Presbyterian Church in Fort Lauderdale. The building was made possible by gifts of members of his church.

Covenant, East Detroit, Mich. (the Rev. David H. McAlpin, pastor), of a new sanctuary.

First, Traverse City, Mich. (the Rev. Donald W. Ferguson, pastor), of a new sanctuary.

Naples, N.Y. (the Rev. Edwin D. Miner, pastor), of a new educational unit.

Park, Newark, N.Y. (the Rev. Walter R. Hobkirk, pastor), of a new pipe organ.

Presbyterian Historical Society, Philadelphia, Pa., of a bronze bust of the late Rev. Alexander Mackie, former president of the Presbyterian Ministers' Fund. The bust will be placed on permanent display in the society's Alexander Mackie Exhibition Hall in recognition of his efforts on behalf of the society's new building.

APPOINTMENTS AND ELECTIONS:

The Reverend Donald P. Buteyn, Berkeley, Calif., to associate executive of the Synod of Washington-Alaska, serving Seattle Presbytery.

PRESBYTERIANS HONORED:

The Reverend Thomas John Carlisle was honored by members and friends of Stone Street Church, Watertown, N. Y., on the completion of twenty years as pastor.

The Reverend Frederick T. Steen was honored by members and friends of Westminster Church, Rogers City, Mich., upon completion of fifteen years as pastor.

July 15, 1969

25

169

ANDREW PERNELL

UNIVERSITY OF ALABAMA
UNIVERSITY, ALABAMA 35486

OFFICE FOR ACADEMIC AFFAIRS

September 3, 1969

Mr. Robert J. Cadigan, Editor
Presbyterian Life Magazine
Wetherspoon Building
Philadelphia, Pennsylvania   19107

Dear Mr. Cadigan:

A recent article in <u>Presbyterian Life</u> (July 15, 1969) by
Wilmina M. Rowland did not include relevant information which
would have prevented the University of Alabama from appearing
to be a racist institution.

A Southeastern Conference (SEC) rule limits the number of
scholarship holders on the football team to a total of 125 students,
at a rate of forty per year. Your correspondent, Andy, joined
the team after this allotted number had been filled. His continuance
on the team while on scholarship would have meant a violation by
Alabama of conference rules, with subsequent penalties.

Since by SEC regulations the candidate could not participate as
a student athlete while receiving financial support, he had to choose
between playing and receiving aid. Fortunately for his education,
he chose the scholarship. Unfortunately for the football team, which
did want him to stay, he could not play.

The real point of Andy's letter to your Student Opportunity
Scholarship office was not to complain about the Alabama athletic
team, but to point out that the scholarship given him last year, and
for which he dropped off the team, was not renewed this year. He
was obviously still in need of aid--and asking for SOS financial
help more than he was asking for a critique of football regulations.
I hope you can help.

Sincerely yours,

Willard F. Gray
Chairman, Faculty Committee
on Intercollegiate Athletics

WFG/ll

bcc: Dr. David Mathews   Mr. W. E. Pickens
     Dr. Larry McGehee   Mr. James Wilder

170

THOMAS, TALIAFERRO, FORMAN, BURR & MURRAY

SIXTEENTH FLOOR BANK FOR SAVINGS BUILDING

BIRMINGHAM, ALABAMA 35203

TELEPHONE 323-7711 AREA CODE 205

ANDREW J. THOMAS
MARK L. TALIAFERRO
JAMES R. FORMAN, JR.
SAMUEL H. BURR
WILLIAM K. MURRAY
A. JACKSON NOBLE, JR.
C. V. STELZENMULLER
ROBERT G. TATE
J. FRED POWELL
SAM W. OLIVER, JR

PAUL O. WOODALL
J. FREDRIC INGRAM
WILLIAM C. KNIGHT, JR.
R. LEE WALTHALL
LOUIS H. ANDERS, JR.
JOSEPH G. STEWART
JOHN D. CLEMENTS
MARK TALIAFERRO, JR.

May 5, 1971

Mr. U. W. Clemon
1630 4th Avenue, North
Birmingham, Alabama 35203

RE: The Afro-American Association, et al
v. Paul "Bear" Bryant, et al
United States District Court
Northern District of Alabama
CA 62-422-W

Dear Mr. Clemon:

Reference is made to your recent conversation with Mr. Knight in our office with reference to the captioned case which is set for pre-trial hearing before Judge McFadden at 10:00 A.M. on Monday, May 10.

According to information which we have received from the Athletic Department of the University of Alabama, the following black athletes were signed to football grants-in-aid during the year 1970-71:

Ralph Stokes, Montgomery, Alabama
Mike Washington, Montgomery, Alabama
John Mitchell, Mobile, Alabama
Sylvester Croom, Tuscaloosa, Alabama

Charles Cleveland, Bibb County High School, Centerville, Alabama, was signed to a basketball grant-in-aid.

During the A-Day game which was played in Tuscaloosa on May 1, John Mitchell played and also Wilbur Jackson. The latter student was signed to a football grant-in-aid and played on the freshman football team during the Fall of 1970. The names of both John Mitchell and Wilbur Jackson appeared in the printed program for said game.

CPSIA information can be obtained
at www.ICGtesting.com
Printed in the USA
LVHW071115270721
693810LV00001B/23